Wise Guy

Also by Guy Kawasaki

The Art of the Start

The Art of the Start 2.0

The Art of Social Media

APE: Author, Publisher, Entrepreneur

Enchantment

What the Plus!

The Macintosh Way

Reality Check

How to Drive Your Competition Crazy

Rules for Revolutionaries

Selling the Dream

Hindsights

The Computer Curmudgeon

Database 101

Wise Guy

Lessons from a Life

Guy

Kawasaki

Portfolio / Penguin

PORTFOLIO/PENGUIN
An imprint of Penguin Random House LLC
penguinrandomhouse.com

Copyright © 2019 by Guy Kawasaki
Penguin supports copyright. Copyright fuels creativity, encourages diverse voices, promotes
free speech, and creates a vibrant culture. Thank you for buying an authorized edition of this
book and for complying with copyright laws by not reproducing, scanning, or distributing any
part of it in any form without permission. You are supporting writers and allowing Penguin to
continue to publish books for every reader.

Page 37: Photo courtesy of Afro Newspaper/Gado/Getty Images.

Most Portfolio books are available at a discount when purchased in quantity for sales
promotions or corporate use. Special editions, which include personalized covers, excerpts, and
corporate imprints, can be created when purchased in large quantities. For more information,
please call (212) 572-2232 or email specialmarkets@penguinrandomhouse.com. Your local
bookstore can also assist with discounted bulk purchases using the Penguin Random House
corporate Business-to-Business program. For assistance in locating a participating retailer,
email B2B@penguinrandomhouse.com.

ISBN 9780525538615 (hardcover)
ISBN 9780525538622 (ebook)

Printed in the United States of America
10 9 8 7 6 5 4 3 2 1

Book design by Lauren Kolm

Penguin is committed to publishing works of quality and integrity. In that spirit, we are
proud to offer this book to our readers; however, the story, the experiences, and the words
are the author's alone.

While the author has made every effort to provide accurate telephone numbers, internet
addresses, and other contact information at the time of publication, neither the publisher nor
the author assumes any responsibility for errors or for changes that occur after publication.
Further, the publisher does not have any control over and does not assume any responsibility
for author or third-party websites or their content.

To my wife, Beth, my greatest source of wisdom

What you leave behind is not
what is engraved in stone monuments,
but what is woven into the lives of others.

—Pericles

Contents

Preface xiii

How This Book Is Organized xv

Mahalo xvii

01. Immigration 1

02. Education 9

03. Inspiration 25

04. Apple 51

05. Business 77

06. Values 105

07. Parenting 131

08. Sports 149

09. LOL 167

10. Skills 187

11. *Ohana* 209

Postpartum 231

Recommended Reading 235

Index 237

Preface

People think that stories are shaped by people.
In fact, it's the other way around.

—Terry Pratchett

Before you ask, or wonder, this is not my autobiography or memoir. It is a compilation of the most enlightening stories of my life. Think personal lessons, not personal history.

My stories do not depict epic, tragic, or heroic occurrences, because that hasn't been the trajectory of my life. They do not depict a rapid, meteoric rise, either. One decision. One failure. Hard work. One success. My goal is to educate, not awe, you.

From the bottom of my heart, I hope my stories help you to live a more joyous, productive, and meaningful life. If *Wise Guy* succeeds at this, then that's the best story of all.

Guy Kawasaki
Silicon Valley, California, 2018

How This Book Is Organized

Consistency is contrary to nature, contrary to life.
The only completely consistent people are the dead.

—Aldous Huxley

The flow of this book is a combination of chronological and topical. It's not purely chronological because acquiring wisdom isn't a quick or linear process.

The format for most of the book is a story followed by the wisdom it represents. I diverge from this format in a few places, and it's important to me that you know that neither sloppy writing nor careless editing caused the inconsistency.

Each nugget of wisdom is marked with the *shaka* symbol, which looks like this: . Shaka is a Hawaiian/surfing hand symbol that loosely translates to "aloha," "right on," or "mahalo," depending on the context.

Lastly, I hate bugs, and after fifteen books, I know that no matter how meticulous an author and publisher are, a few might sneak through. Please send me an email at GuyKawasaki@gmail.com to report errors that you find, as well as—even better—provide your feedback about the book.

Mahalo

*Feeling gratitude and not expressing it is like
wrapping a present and not giving it.*

—William Arthur Ward

Jennifer Barr, Courtney Colwell, David Deal, Marylene Delbourg-Delphis, Moira Gunn, Bruna Martinuzzi, Terri Mayall, Will Mayall, Craig "Big Wave" Stein, Kirsten Tanner, and Shawn Welch helped with the initial conceptualization of the book.

Rick Kot provided the deft touch that guided me editorially. Rainer Hosch and Marc Silber took the great photos that adorn the dust jacket. Christopher Sergio then created a great dust jacket with them. Norma Barksdale made everything work together.

Cathy Chong, Lori Couderc, and Suzan Liggett provided irreplaceable assistance with background information and fact-checking. There's nothing like writing a book to discover how little you know!

These people volunteered to read and comment on early drafts. They found more than a thousand ways to make the book better:

Michael Bomhoff

Kris Bondi

Susan Bouvette

Bukanla Boyd

Stephen Brand

Buzz Bruggeman

S. Chowdhary

Karen Coppock

Jerry Crisci

Tom Curtis

Benoît H. Dicaire

Glendalynn Dixon

Papasavvas Elias

Andres Elizalde

Doug Erickson

Teresa Esola

Hendrik Eybers

Rob Ferguson

Daniel Fryda

Cailey Gibson

Roger Haller

Pérez Herrera

Abdul Jaleel

Jennifer J. Johnson

Beth Kawasaki

Nic Kawasaki

Dori Kemker

Swati Khurana

Ruth Lund

Todd Lyden

Svetlana Maklakova

Chuck Marecic

Howard Miller

Donna Mills

Kimberly Moore

Leslie Morgan Nakajima

Randee Napp

Ryan O'Mara

Cory Ondrejka

Anitha Pai

Santino Pasutto

Klemen Peternel

Emily-Anne Pillari

Matthias Rönsberg

Sérgio Rosa

Jadeep Shah

Parker Sipes

Patrick Slattery

Naga Subramanya   *Pérez Herrera Walevska*

Maja Vujovic   *Lisa Westby*

Dan Waite   *Bill Whiteside*

Stack's Menlo Park, Stack's Redwood City, Coffeebar Menlo Park, Cat and Cloud, Cliff Café, Verve, Kaito, Harbor Café, East Side Eatery, and The Buttery provided crucial places to eat, drink, and work.

A big MAHALO to you all.

Wise
Guy

Immigration

Yes, we can. It was sung by immigrants as they struck out from distant shores and pioneers who pushed westward against an unforgiving wilderness.

—Barack Obama

I come from a long line of dreamers. My story starts with my grandparents' emigration from Japan to Hawaii in order to pursue a better life for themselves and their children. I need to spend a few pages on this history because everything flows from their decision.

My Father's Side

My great-grandparents on my father's side immigrated to Hawaii from Hiroshima between 1890 and 1900. This was near the end of the Meiji period, when there were two major conflicts: the First Sino-Japanese War and the Russo-Japanese War. At the time, young Japanese men were required to serve in the military.

Instead, my great-grandparents immigrated to Hawaii and worked as contract laborers for the Hakalau Plantation Company, fifteen miles north of Kona, on the Big Island. Thus, you could make the case that I come from a family of draft dodgers. It is safer, after all, to harvest sugar in Hawaii than to invade China or Russia. However, the pay was $1 per day. Still, that choice was a no-brainer.

Back row, left to right: Harold Kawasaki (uncle), Duke Kawasaki (father), Harry Tomita (grand uncle), and Richard Kawasaki (uncle). Front row, left to right: Mildred Harada (aunt), Yonetaro Kawasaki (grandfather), and Katherine Haruo (grand aunt).

Eventually, my great-grandparents moved to Honolulu from the Big Island. They had three children: my grandmother, Alma, plus

Katherine and Harry. These siblings were the first generation of American Kawasakis, because Hawaii was a territory of the United States at the time. Their education did not go beyond the eighth grade.

In Honolulu, Alma married Yonetaro Kawasaki, and they had five children: my father, Duke, plus my aunt (Mildred) and uncles (Harry, Harold, and Richard). According to the 1940 federal census, Yonetaro was an unemployed chauffeur—this may explain my love of cars, which you'll read about later. He may also have been on an FBI watch list because he traveled to and from Japan using two different names.

Alma died from childbirth complications. At the age of nineteen, my great-aunt, Katherine, took over Alma's maternal duties while also working as a housekeeper. This meant she was the mother to four kids between the ages of two and ten years old. As I grew up, she was effectively my grandmother on my father's side.

Incidentally, Katherine set me on a lifelong path of kindness to animals. When I was in elementary school, I killed a *mejiro* bird with a

BB gun; this breed of bird had emigrated from Japan, too. Katherine made me feel terrible for shooting it. I haven't killed another animal other than rats and fish since that day— though you'll learn about my role in a wild boar hunt later.

My father started working at age fourteen to support the family. He graduated from high school but did not get a college degree. He did, however, attend the Berklee College of Music in Boston for a short time.

My parents' wedding photo.

As a teenager my dad loved music.

He played the piano, saxophone, flute, and clarinet. He even started a jazz band called Duke Kawa's and became friends with Guy Lombardo, the famous bandleader from Canada. In honor of this friendship, my parents named me Guy. Fortunately, they didn't name me after Guy's brother Carmen.

Left to right: Carmen Lombardo, my father,
Guy Lombardo (my namesake), and my mother.

My father was an intelligent and passionate man who loved to read. The shelves in our house were filled with classics, plus the *World Book Encyclopedia*. He often told me that we would always have money to buy books. Both my parents realized that not getting a college education limited one's earning potential and options in life. Due to the constraints they encountered, they placed a huge emphasis on education for my sister, Jean, and me.

My father later became a stevedore and then a fireman, and because there were long periods when there was nothing to do, he studied to become a real estate agent. Then, his deep sense of civic duty led him into politics. He ran for the Hawaii state senate three times before he was elected. He remained a senator for approximately twenty years.

He was a hard-core liberal who wanted to help the "common man." For example, he created the Office of the Ombudsman to investigate the complaints of citizens about the actions of the executive branch agencies of the state and county governments. On the day of his memorial service, the flags of the state government flew at half-mast.

My Mother's Side

My grandfather on my mother's side, Chikao Hirabayashi, was born in Japan in 1893. My maternal grandmother, Tomoyo Jike, was born in Kohala, Hawaii, in 1898. They had seven children: my mother, Lucy, plus Jean, Elsie, Marian, Richard, Ellen, and Harriet.

Like my father, my mother did not attend college. Her family, however, was wealthy, so she went to Yokohama, Japan, in 1939 for schooling. Fortunately, she returned to Hawaii on one of the last two ships before the Japanese attack on Pearl Harbor in 1941.

My mother was a homemaker who dedicated her life to our family. I have eaten all over the world, and nothing compares to her beef stew, guava ice cakes, and *tsukemono* (pickled vegetables). At less than five feet tall, she was tiny but strong. She, not my father, taught me not to take crap from anyone.

My mother loved my sister, Jean, and me with all her heart and showed it by dedicating her adult life to our happiness. She also taught me one thing that I've carried throughout my life: the mandate to "always leave a place neater than you found it." This is why I am a neat freak, if not borderline obsessive-compulsive.

Growing Up in Hawaii

My family lived in Kalihi Valley, a poor part of Honolulu. If you've traveled from Honolulu International Airport to Kaneohe through the Wilson Tunnel, you've driven right past my childhood home. At the time, working-class Hawaiians, Filipinos, Samoans, Japanese, and Chinese lived in Kalihi Valley.

My childhood home in Kalihi Valley. This photo was taken after a massive remodeling. It never looked this good when I lived there.

There were few Caucasians, whom locals pejoratively call *haoles*. Our neighbors worked as clerks, janitors, and laborers—if they were employed at all. Our house was near a public housing project. I didn't venture into it because most of the residents were Hawaiians and Samoans, and I was Japanese American. You didn't go into that housing project if you were a Japanese American kid.

My sister, Jean Okimoto, is four years older than I am. She got the artistic talents in our family, including the ability to transform pieces of paper into objects of art—also known as origami. I freely admit that she has a higher level of intellectual ability than I do.

I had a happy childhood in the paradise and melting pot that is Hawaii. I did not struggle against poverty or prejudice. My life was good because my parents worked hard, didn't take much for themselves, and always invested in their kids' futures.

My family, circa 1972. This picture was taken at the state capitol building where my father served as a state senator.

Wisdom

Change a losing game. Don't stand by the side of the river waiting for a roast duck to fly into your mouth (as the Chinese proverb goes). Take action. Make decisions. Change a losing situation, or one that's going nowhere. In other words, move to a country, state, city, or neighborhood that has more opportunities.

Moving to Hawaii changed everything for my family. If my grandparents hadn't made that decision, I would be a "salary man" working for a large company in Japan. Or I wouldn't exist at all, because my father's family lived in Hiroshima during World War II.

Were it not for the opportunities, education, and upward mobility that America afforded, the life of every subsequent generation of my family might have been different because of the limited opportunities in Japan. My family and I owe everything to America.

🤙 Remember the opportunities that you were afforded. After you've "made it," provide opportunities to others. In doing so, you honor the people who came before you by helping the people who come after you.

🤙 Document your family's history while your parents and grandparents are alive. Reconstructing my own family's history was difficult, and there are major gaps in the information that I compiled. Ancestry.com is a good resource, but it's not perfect.

02

Education

My life is proof of a fundamental truth: education is a great catalyst and equalizer. My education, made possible by my parents' sacrifices, began in a poor part of Honolulu and ended in Los Angeles, California, with a crucial stop in Palo Alto, California, along the way.

One Person Can Make a Difference

I went to a public school called Kalihi Elementary—the yellow buildings on the *ewa* (west) side of Likelike Highway. My educational path

Kalihi Elementary School.

would typically have taken me from Kalihi Elementary to Kalakaua Middle School to Farrington High School to the University of Hawaii. After college I would have worked in a retail, tourism, or agricultural job.

Akau's advice changed the trajectory of my life.

However, that was not my path, because my sixth-grade schoolteacher, Trudy Akau, told my parents that I had too much potential to remain in the public school system. She insisted that I apply to private, college-prep schools—specifically, Punahou and 'Iolani.

Punahou is the school that President Barack Obama attended. I went to 'Iolani. It was eight miles from our house, and it cost $1,250 per year, which, adjusted for inflation, is equivalent to $8,000 in 2018. Given my parents' modest income of approximately $20,000 per year, this was a large sum of money for them to scrape together.

Akau's advice changed the trajectory of my life. If she had not convinced my parents to send me to 'Iolani, I would not have gone to Stanford. If I had not gone to Stanford, I would not have met the guy who got me interested in computers and gave me a job at Apple.

Wisdom

Be a Trudy Akau. Take an interest in others, help them, go outside your comfort zone, and share advice with them and their families. One caring person changed the course of my life. You could do the same.

Accept the advice of people like Trudy Akau. Teachers, coaches, counselors, and ministers do what they do because they want to help others. They usually have your best interests at heart. Listen to them.

Thank the Trudy Akaus in your life before it's too late. I never expressed my gratitude to her because she died before I understood how much influence she had on my life. Not thanking her is one of the greatest regrets I have.

Understand that you are, in the words of Steve Jobs, "denting the universe" if you are a teacher, coach, pastor, priest, rabbi, or hold a position that influences people. You may affect only one person at a time and only a few over your lifetime, but every dent counts.

Make no mistake: you are doing God's work.

The Toughest Teachers Are the Best

Before you read this section, think about the best teachers you had in your life—at any time, in any subject. Go to that place in your mind, and you'll get the full impact of what I'm about to tell you.

At the age of fourteen, I entered the seventh grade at 'Iolani. This was a private Episcopalian college-prep school that provided instruction from kindergarten through the twelfth grade. When I attended, it was an all-boys school with a graduating class of 150 students.

Looking back, 'Iolani was a great experience. There were many teachers (Charles Proctor, Joseph Yelas, John Kay, Dan Feldhaus, and Lucille Bratcher), coaches (Edward Hamada, Charles Kaaihue, and Bob Barry), and staff members (William Lee and David Coon) who taught me how to think, how to work hard, and how to be part of a team.

Although I thought I did well in high school, I found my ninth-grade English report card when doing research for this book. It's pictured here; talk about selective memory! Somehow, luckily, I got through Honors English and into Advanced Placement English and became a student of Harold Keables.

My ninth-grade English report card. I'm glad I found this *after* the fifteenth book, or I might not have become an author.

Of the 'Iolani faculty and staff, Keables had the greatest impact on me. He was my AP English teacher—and the toughest teacher I had at any level of education. He was the most demanding, and he taught me the most. (There's a causal relationship there.)

Harold Keables, my English teacher in high school.

I hope you have a Harold Keables at least once in your life. He taught me to hold myself to high standards and the value of hard work. For example, here's how he taught writing:

- He circled the errors that you made in your essay.
- You copied the sentence as you originally wrote it.
- You cited and quoted the rule that you violated from *Good Writing: An Informal Manual of Style* by Alan Vrooman.
- You rewrote the sentence correctly.
- You turned this in as homework and hoped you got it right the second time.

This was the 1970s—long before personal computers and word processing, so we wrote everything out in cursive, using a pen. When every error involved a three-step process to correct, you learned the rules of grammar and spelling after only a few papers. Keables is the reason I acquired a disdain for the passive voice and a love of the serial comma.

Eventually I read *The Chicago Manual of Style* from cover to cover, because Keables inspired such attention to detail. In the final editing of my books, also thanks to his influence, I go on a rampage with Microsoft Word's search function:

- "Be" is a smoking gun for the passive voice, and the passive voice is weak. To be is not to be.
- "Very" is imprecise—how much is "very"? How dark is very dark? How fast is very fast? How scary is very scary? How good is a writer who is dependent on "very"? Not very.
- Adverbs are for wimps, so I purge words that end in "ly." How quick is quickly? How smooth is smoothly? How rich is richly?
- "Kind of" is not an approximation. It is a type of or an example of—for example, a hibiscus is a kind of flower, but it's not "kind of" (moderately) pretty.

. . . you can't measure the impact of a teacher until at least twenty years have passed . . .

You were the Man, Harold Keables!

Wisdom

Seek out and embrace people who challenge you. You will learn more from them than from the folks who hold you to lower standards. When you look back years later, you will realize that the toughest teachers and bosses were the ones who taught you the most. Iron sharpens iron.

Keables and Steve Jobs are both in this category for me. (There's much more to come about Steve.) Were it not for these two people, my expectations of myself, and therefore my accomplishments, would have been lower.

Be a hard-ass if you are a teacher, manager, coach, or someone who influences people. You're not doing anyone a favor by lowering your standards and expectations in an effort to be kind, gentle, or popular. The future cost of short-term kindness is great.

Be patient. I wasn't one of Keables's best students, so he's probably now in heaven, amazed that I'm the one who has written fifteen books. If you're a teacher, you never know which student is going to internalize what you taught and run with it. It may take a while—you can't measure the impact of a teacher until at least twenty years have passed—but it can happen.

Thank the people who helped you achieve results before they are gone, as I advised regarding Trudy Akau. You'll regret not doing so if the opportunity passes.

A Little Fear Is Good

Three other youthful experiences taught me to respect adults and to not screw around. The first occurred on a Kalihi Elementary field trip to the Nike (nothing to do with the shoe company) missile site in Kahuku, Hawaii.

After the tour, the army served us lunch, and I dropped a clump of rice on the floor. I picked it up and was about to throw it back on the floor when an army officer, in an intimidating, authoritative, drill sergeant voice, said, "Don't throw that on the floor. Pick it up and bus your tray." He scared the crap out of me, and from that day forward I respected people in uniforms.

The second formative incident occurred when my father took me to his workplace, the alarm bureau of the Honolulu Fire Department. This facility dispatched fire trucks when people reported a fire.

While waiting for him one day after school, I activated an alarm box to see what would happen. The box was there for demonstrations, but I didn't know that. My father convinced me that I had caused firemen to jump down the pole into a fire truck and rush to a fire.

He also told me that it was a crime to make a false alarm, so the police might come for me. He and his buddies had a good laugh, but the experience made me a scaredy-cat who didn't push back against the rules. This lesson probably kept me out of much teenage-boy reptilian-brain trouble.

The third experience took place at 'Iolani. The only time I got into trouble in high school was when I convinced a buddy to cut art class with me. Stupidly, we picked the day that a handful of other students did the same thing.

We all got detention, and in my case, the punishment was sweeping the basketball gym floor for a week. This experience, unlike the previous two, didn't scare me, but it was an important lesson because it was embarrassing. And I hate being embarrassed.

My parents also gave me hell for doing this. After all, they were making a big investment in my education. Back then, there weren't many doting helicopter parents (the kind who "hover" over their kids to protect them). The teacher was always right. You did what he or she said. End of discussion. This sounds archaic now, but the "teacher as all-powerful" approach worked on me.

Wisdom

Teach people to respect authority. Contrary to the mania for building supportive, nurturing, and protected environments to supposedly maximize self-esteem, creativity, and confidence, scaring the crap out of people can be a good thing. Sometimes you should just listen and obey, not question and debate.

The World Isn't Black and White

Ever since I was young, my parents developed a sense of honesty and honor in me. I learned that it was disgraceful to lie, cheat, or steal. But one day that value system was rocked when my favorite uncle took me shopping at a department store called Wigwam, now long gone, to get some screws to repair his house.

He opened a plastic container in the store, took a few screws, and left. My uncle was a shoplifter, and I was his accomplice! The explanation he gave me was that he needed only a few and didn't want to buy a full container, but this was still wrong.

He was totally honest and fair in everything else I saw him do. He was my favorite uncle because he took me to the movies and the zoo. Even today, I still struggle to make sense of why he stole those screws.

Wisdom

Accept that people aren't good or bad. Good people can do bad things, and bad people can do good things. This includes yourself—you will do bad things that you will regret. Thus, the ability to cope with contradictions, paradoxes, and discontinuities is an important skill.

This ability is called "aintegration," a term coined by Jacob Lomranz of the School of Psychological Sciences and the Herczeg Institute on Aging, Tel Aviv University, and Yael Benyamini of the Bob Shapell School of Social Work, Tel Aviv University.

Google this title to read more about aintegration: "The Ability to Live with Incongruence: Aintegration—The Concept and Its Operationalization." The key to aintegration is that it prevents you from going down the slippery slope to the "dark side." In my case, that would have been, "If my uncle does something like this, it's okay for me, too."

Remember that you are influencing people who are watching you. The transgression that you consider inconsequential could shape the values and morals of others without your ever knowing it—but so could your kindness and generosity.

I am confident that if my uncle had been aware of the impact this small act would have on me, he would have purchased the full container of screws.

Father Knows Best

Dan Feldhaus was a great math teacher and college counselor at 'Iolani. He must have seen something in me, because he convinced me to apply to Stanford. To my surprise, I was accepted. The only explanation is that in the early 1970s, Asian Americans were considered an oppressed minority, so my race got me admitted.

My grade point average was 3.4, and my SAT scores were 610 for math and 680 for English. These were good, but not great, scores. No tutors helped me improve my grade point average, and no consultants helped me polish my essays. I didn't visit any colleges (even the University of Hawaii, two miles from 'Iolani).

In 2018, Stanford won't even read your application unless you have a 4.2 GPA, 2400 on the SATs, and a Nobel Prize for starting a nonprofit—unless your family donated a building. There is no chance that I would get into Stanford in 2018.

Don't get me wrong: I wasn't a total loser. I did win the scholar-athlete award at 'Iolani for the class of 1972. I also won the athlete-scholar award, which I shared with a classmate named Mufi Hannemann. (These are two different awards: with an emphasis on scholastic over athletic or athletic over scholastic excellence.) He went on to Harvard, won a Fulbright scholarship, and became the mayor of Honolulu.

The University of Hawaii (UH), Occidental, and Stanford accepted me. (I applied to more colleges, but I can't remember which ones!) I loved playing football and could have played at Occidental, so my first choice was the school that Barack

> **"I'm not paying for a school so you can play football."**

Obama made famous. (He supposedly got a B in the politics class of Professor Roger Boesche.)

But my father made the decision for me: "If I'm going to pay all this money, you're going to Stanford. Or you can go to UH for free. I'm not paying for a school so you can play football." So much for fostering independent thinking in your children. I went to Stanford.

By the way, Stanford tuition back in 1972 was $2,850 per year. It was $62,000 per year in 2018. My father loved to go to Las Vegas to shoot craps. I would join him and my mother there once every few months throughout my Stanford career. There were many times when I paid my tuition with $100 bills from Las Vegas.

Wisdom

Don't let people make mistakes. At least play the devil's advocate and explain why they might be making one. I wanted to go to Occidental to play football, because, after all, that's a smart way to pick a college. Not! That would have been a stupid decision.

My father was right to coerce me into attending Stanford. If there were good reasons for me to attend a small liberal arts school such as Occidental, then *fine*; but playing football was not on the list of "good reasons."

I'm not saying that going to Stanford was either necessary or sufficient for me to succeed. Nor am I saying that I would not have succeeded had I gone to Occidental. But there's no doubt that going to Stanford shaped my career because of the people I met there.

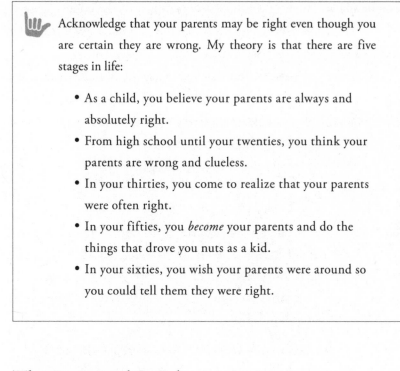

Acknowledge that your parents may be right even though you are certain they are wrong. My theory is that there are five stages in life:

- As a child, you believe your parents are always and absolutely right.
- From high school until your twenties, you think your parents are wrong and clueless.
- In your thirties, you come to realize that your parents were often right.
- In your fifties, you *become* your parents and do the things that drove you nuts as a kid.
- In your sixties, you wish your parents were around so you could tell them they were right.

The Promised Land

'Iolani was the first educational institution that changed my life. Stanford was the second. That experience began in the fall of 1972, when I got off a Western Airlines flight from Honolulu, jumped into a van for incoming freshmen, and rode to the Stanford campus for the first time.

I had no idea what to expect when the van stopped, but I learned fast. California was the promised land: exotic cars, blond girls, moderate weather, and tech companies where people made lots of money. I did not get homesick or suffer from the freshman blues. The skies parted, and the angels sang. This was where God intended for me to be.

It was at Stanford that I met Mike Boich, who became the first software evangelist of Apple's Macintosh Division. We were both then sophomores and hit it off immediately because of a shared love of cars. Ten years later, Boich hired me at Apple, and that's how my technology career kicked into high gear.

Those were formative years that raised my goals and expectations beyond a career in retail, tourism, or agriculture in Hawaii. Had I not left Hawaii, my life would have taken a very different path, and I would not have accomplished all that I have.

Wisdom

Go away for college if you can. Change your surroundings. Embrace the unknown and resist the known. Going to college across the Pacific Ocean—2,336 miles away—was a horizon-expanding, exciting, and fun experience that taught me many important lessons:

- No matter how awesome you were at Podunk High, there's always someone smarter, bigger, or faster than you. For example, I tried out for the Stanford football team and quit after two days. I surmised that college football was a different game, and my goal was not to be a Japanese "Rudy," the diminutive and unqualified kid who played football for Notre Dame in the 1970s.
- However, if you eliminate the outliers who are smarter, bigger, and faster, a kid from Kalihi Valley could still compete with most of the best and brightest at Stanford. Yes, there were Olympic athletes, child prodigies, and the offspring of billionaires, but most students were similar in capabilities, aspirations, and expectations. Don't be intimidated by your classmates.

- There are other ways that your path becomes clear. I went on rounds at the Stanford Medical Center because I had delusions of becoming a doctor. On the first day, I fainted, and I interpreted my collapse as a message that I wasn't meant to be a doctor. I doubt that I would have passed organic chemistry anyway.
- Japanese Americans from the mainland were different from Japanese Americans from Hawaii. Specifically, they felt oppressed by whites. Coming from Hawaii, I didn't know that I was oppressed and that I should be pissed off. I hadn't even heard of the internment of Japanese Americans during World War II. As someone from Hawaii, it was inconceivable that "dumb *haoles*" could boss around Japanese Americans.
- My God, California girls were beautiful. The transition from an all-boys school in Hawaii to Stanford was shocking.

It's easy for me to say because it's not my money, but if you can afford it, go away for college. The minimum optimal distance is "too far to go home to do laundry"—even if it's just a different part of the same state, province, or country.

As you make decisions in your life, more data is better than less, so traveling, living away from home, and meeting people with different backgrounds are all valuable. I am grateful for many things my parents did, but sending me to Stanford is at the top of my list.

03

Inspiration

We are all in the gutter, but some of us
are looking at the stars.

—Oscar Wilde

Awe-inspiring dreams along the lines of world peace, human rights, and ending poverty weren't what stoked my ambitions and drove me to succeed. My goals were simple and proletarian but highly motivating nonetheless.

Inspiration Comes from Many Sources

My father loved Cadillacs. I can remember our family owning three Sedan DeVilles over the course of my youth. This was during Cadillac's glory days—long before German cars became the de facto automotive status symbol.

Caddys back then were big, powerful, and air-conditioned, and the seats were covered with leather instead of cloth. We may have lived in a poor area, but that doesn't mean my parents didn't work hard to buy a few nice things.

Prior to our Cadillac days, my father drove a Toyota Corona, and I hated it. The Corona drove like it was made of melted beer cans, and it was underpowered, even for Honolulu's low-speed streets. I hated being seen in it and later hated driving it.

In retrospective amazement, let me tell you that my father let me use his Cadillac for dates. It was fantastic for a kid from Kalihi Valley, who was attending 'Iolani with rich Asians and *haoles*, to take dates out in a Cadillac. Note to parents: let your kids use your car for dates—especially if you have a nice car.

> **While some heroes strived to "change the world," I only wanted to "change the car."**

In my teenage years, I decided I was not going to drive a crappy car, and this drove me (pun intended) to study and work hard. Shallow as this sounds, it's the truth. While some heroes strived to "change the world," I only wanted to "change the car."

At Stanford my teenage passion for cars became a permanent part of my persona. For example, I loved parents' weekends. The families of my friends would swoop in and take us to eat at a Chinese restaurant called Ming's. The chicken salad was to die for, and a welcome change from dorm food.

More important, many parents who drove to Stanford had a positive effect on me. They often pulled up in exotic cars as I played basketball outside a dorm called Soto. The game would stop, and someone would usually say (and everyone would think), "Someday, I want to drive a car like that."

In particular, I remember Dr. Nobuyuki Kawata, a cardiologist from Los Angeles who pioneered heart transplants at the UCLA Medical Center. His daughter Carol was the sweetest girl you could ever meet; she later became a successful doctor herself in the Los Angeles area.

Dr. Kawata drove a metallic-blue Ferrari 275 GTB, and if you think my father's Cadillac was a big influence, you can imagine what Dr. Kawata's Ferrari did for my aspirations. His car (as well as Asian American parental preferences) was why I considered a medical career—until I heard how hard organic chemistry was and had my fainting episode at Stanford Medical Center.

One final car story: Mike Boich, the Stanford classmate who ultimately hired me to work at Apple, once invited me to his family's home in Phoenix, Arizona. The backyard of his house was the golf course of

Mike Boich's mother's Ferrari Daytona.

the Arizona Biltmore Hotel. He lived on a golf course! This was a long way from Kalihi Valley.

One night after dinner at the hotel, Boich's mother asked me to drive her home in her Ferrari Daytona while Boich's father took his Rolls-Royce. My head exploded: so *this* is how rich people live!

Wisdom

👍 Don't worry about what motivates you. What's important is that you *are* motivated. Something as materialistic as cars inspired me. More power to you if your goals are lofty, but there are many sources of motivation.

👍 Provide inspiration to others, too. Over the years, several car manufacturers loaned me cars to drive. I took my kids for rides in these cars, and I let my older kids drive them (contrary to the loan agreements). I also took my kids' friends (hey, Giselle!) and the kids of my friends (hey, Kai!) for rides because I hoped this exposure would motivate them as much as it had inspired me.

One Book Can Change Your Life

In 1987, my wife gave me a copy of a book called *If You Want to Write* by Brenda Ueland, a writing professor at the University of Minnesota.

It has influenced me more than any other book that I've read, and I've been recommending it for thirty years. Thousands of people read it because of my recommendation, and no one has given me negative feedback. Its essence is that if you want to write, don't listen to the critics and naysayers—especially your *internal* critic and naysayer.

Just write! You don't need training, permission, or approval. Just write!

If You Want to Write empowered me to think freely, creatively, and boldly. Though I was not an "author" in anyone's mind, including my own, it enabled me to write my first book, *The Macintosh Way*. It helped me become a writer by removing the limitations I placed on myself. Here are four quotations from *If You Want to Write* to whet your appetite for reading it:

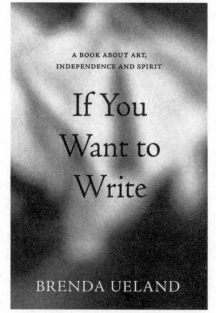

A BOOK ABOUT ART, INDEPENDENCE AND SPIRIT

If You Want to Write

BRENDA UELAND

If You Want to Write, by Brenda Ueland

- "Everyone is talented, original, and has something important to say."
- "Be careless, reckless! Be a lion, be a pirate, when you want to write."
- "Women should neglect their housework to write."
- "You do not know what is in you . . ."

But the book's impact went far beyond my writing career and influenced my approach to life. The title is *If You Want to Write,* but you can substitute any creative endeavor and most professions for the word "write." For example, if you want to develop software, if you want to start a company, if you want to make movies, if you want to paint, if you want to play music. If you want to do almost anything . . .

Read *If You Want to Write*. Full stop. There is no greater recommendation than an author's urging you to read a book that he did not write. I am living proof that this book can change a person's life.

The Power of Other People's Success

Sandra Kurtzig is the founder of a company called ASK Group. She earned a math degree from UCLA in 1968, and she was one of the few female engineering students at Stanford. After earning her aeronautical engineering master's degree, Kurtzig went to work for General Electric, where she sold computer time-sharing. She left this position to start ASK Group in a spare bedroom. Hard work and great timing led to ASK's going public in 1981. Kurtzig's share of the company was worth $67 million at the time.

Sometime in the mid-1980s, I got to know Kurtzig through my evangelism job at Apple. She was having trouble with her Macintosh, so I went to her house to provide tech support.

I was familiar with Quicken, so I knew exactly where to look for the current balance.

I've never told anyone this story, but when I sat down to work on her Mac, she had Quicken, a checkbook program, running. Its window was front and center on the screen. I was familiar with Quicken, so I knew exactly where to look for the current balance, and I couldn't resist doing so.

It was $250,000. Yes, she had $250,000 in her checking account. I was blown away. I walked out of her house with a new benchmark: to someday have at least $250,000 in my checking account. Yes, this was another superficial and materialistic goal, but it was highly effective nonetheless.

Wisdom

Embrace the inspiration of people's success. I didn't begrudge Kurtzig for her wealth. Quite the contrary—it showed me what a hardworking entrepreneur could achieve. Until then, I was happy if my bank balance wasn't negative.

I don't suggest prying into people's bank accounts, but the financial success of others can inspire you. That said, ignore people who inherited their wealth. They did little beyond winning the birth lottery. But self-made, successful people are evidence that you can excel, too. Embrace this attitude: "If she/he can do it, so can I."

Crime Can Pay

I was a victim of crime twice in high school. In both cases a *moke* stole money from me. *Moke* is the Hawaiian word for a delinquent, criminal, or tough guy, typically of Hawaiian or Pacific Island ancestry. It rhymes with "stoke" and "bloke" but not "*poke*," the raw fish dish, which rhymes with "okay."

The first crime occurred at a bus stop in front of Kaimuki High School, a public school across the street from 'Iolani. As I was waiting for a bus to go home, a big *moke* came up to me and demanded money. My loss was a few dollars—and my self-esteem.

The second crime occurred in front of Farrington High School, three miles from my house in Kalihi Valley. Another *moke* demanded

The scene of the crime when I was robbed at Kaimuki High School.

money from me as I sat on a public bus. He was smaller than the *moke* in the first story, but intimidating nonetheless. The total take was again a few dollars and my self-esteem. More than forty years later, I would recognize this guy if I ever saw him.

My experiences were mild compared to what many kids go through, because I was not in serious physical danger. But they were scary for me all the same. I hated the fear and intimidation I felt. Ever since those incidents, I've avoided public transportation, and I consider myself a coward for not fighting back.

Wisdom

Turn bad experiences into something good. Getting robbed, albeit in a minor manner, motivated me to study in school and to work hard after graduating.

I never wanted to ride a bus again, and I didn't want to live in a high-crime area. I'm not recommending getting robbed as a source of motivation, but bettering my living environment because of these experiences motivated me.

All Asians Don't Look Alike

Circa 1990. At a stoplight on El Camino Real in Menlo Park, California, I looked to my left and saw a car with four teenage girls in it. They were smiling, giggling, and making eye contact with me.

Smugness ensued.

These girls could have recognized me for many reasons: my work at Apple, my books, my speeches, my hot start-up, or maybe (wishful thinking) my looks. In any case, I thought I had truly arrived: even teenage girls knew who I was.

The girl in the front passenger seat motioned for me to roll down my window, and, being the approachable person I am, I did. She then leaned out of her window and asked, "Are you Jackie Chan?"

> "Are you Jackie Chan?"

I could only shake my head and laugh. So much for being famous. I was just another Asian, albeit one who looked like a *famous* Asian.

On a similar note, in the fall of 2016, I bought a carbon-fiber paddleboard made by Starboard—to be precise, a 10-foot-long, 34-inch-wide model called the Whopper. To celebrate the purchase, I live-broadcasted the unboxing of the board at Covewater Paddle Surf, the store where I bought it.

Two days later I was paddleboarding at Pleasure Point in Santa Cruz. A guy pulled up to me, also on a paddleboard, and asked, "Are

Standing next to the Jackie Chan figure at Madame Tussauds in Beijing.
I'm on the right.

you Guy Kawasaki?" I told him I was, and he said, "I recognized your
board from your live video. I didn't really recognize you."

Wisdom

 Don't flatter yourself. We're all specks of dust in the universe—
it's just that my speck looks like Jackie Chan and my paddle-
board was memorable.

Since the day that teenager asked me if I was Jackie Chan,
one of my goals is that Jackie Chan will be stopped at an intersection in Hong Kong, look over from his Bentley, and see a car
of teenage girls trying to make eye contact with him. Then one
of them will motion for him to roll down his window, and when
he does, she will ask, "Are you Guy Kawasaki?"

Everyone should have goals.

It's Not Personal

In 1994, my wife, first son, and I were living in San Francisco on Union Street, a block from the Presidio, in an area called Cow Hollow. It is one of the most prestigious neighborhoods in San Francisco—I had come a long way from Kalihi Valley.

One day I was trimming the bougainvilleas in front of my house when a white woman in her fifties came up

"Do you also do lawns?"

to me and said, "You're doing such a good job. Do you also do lawns?"

The bougainvilleas that I trimmed as a homeowner, not a gardener.

I assumed her logic was that I was a Japanese man doing yard work in an expensive part of San Francisco, so I was the yardman. I responded to her, "Oh, you think I'm a gardener because I'm Japanese."

She flinched and backtracked with an alternate explanation: "Oh, no, you were doing such a great job that I just thought I'd ask because I need my lawn trimmed." Nice try, lady.

But the point of this anecdote is not racial profiling—quite the contrary.

My father visited me from Hawaii a few weeks later, and I told him the story. Recall that he was a second-generation Japanese American who served in the US Army during World War II. Thus, I expected him to go off in an indignant rage.

But to my surprise, his response was, "Mathematically, in your neighborhood, she was right, so get over it." His statement had a profound effect on how I dealt with people for the rest of my life.

Wisdom

 My father's response taught me five lessons:

- Don't look for problems.
- Take the high road.
- See humor where others see insults.
- Give people the benefit of the doubt—that is, maybe race didn't have anything to do with her question.
- Don't let people get to you, whether they are insulting you or not.

Ever since that day, it's been hard to insult and offend me, and life is easier if you do not take offense easily.

You're Not a Victim

Along the lines of my gardening encounter, Condoleezza Rice, the former secretary of state for George W. Bush, inspired me when I interviewed her for my book *Hindsights*.

Police dog attacking a protester in Birmingham, Alabama. March 1963.

At the time, she was the provost of Stanford University. She was born in Birmingham, Alabama, in 1954 and grew up in Tuscaloosa.

This was during the period when Birmingham's commissioner of public safety, Bull Connor, used fire hoses and police dogs to enforce racial segregation. His brutality helped lead to the passage of the Civil Rights Act of 1964.

Rice told me that you should never consider yourself a victim because then you'll start acting like a victim.

> . . . you should never consider yourself a victim because then you'll start acting like a victim.

You'll begin to believe that you are not in control of your fate and that others are responsible for your welfare. As a result, you develop a dependency on others for your happiness, well-being, and success—thus giving up control of your destiny.

Rice said that if you're going to succeed, you cannot adopt a victim mind-set. You must believe that you control your own fate. No one else is responsible for your success or failure. Her insights had a profound effect on who I believed was responsible for my happiness—that is, me.

Wisdom

👍 Don't consider yourself a victim. Rice clearly overcame much more racism than being asked if she mowed lawns. If you believe you're a victim, you'll truly become one.

👍 Take responsibility for your fate. You still may not succeed, but at least you'll try.

If Condoleezza Rice from Birmingham, Alabama, and Guy Kawasaki from Kalihi Valley, Hawaii, can succeed, you can, too—but not if you believe you're a victim.

👍 Read *Mindset: The New Psychology of Success* by Carol Dweck. It may change how you approach life and how you raise your kids . . . that's all I'm going to tell you about the book.

UPDATED EDITION

CAROL S. DWECK, Ph.D.

mindset
THE NEW PSYCHOLOGY OF SUCCESS

HOW WE CAN
LEARN TO FULFILL
OUR POTENTIAL

2 MILLION COPIES IN PRINT

*parenting
*business
*school
*relationships

"Through clever research studies and engaging writing, Dweck illuminates how our beliefs about our capabilities exert tremendous influence on how we learn and which paths we take in life."
—BILL GATES, *GatesNotes*

Anything Is Possible

A contact lens once popped out of my eye while I was swimming in my pool, and I decided to try to find it. This wasn't a trivial task, since a residential swimming pool contains approximately 14,000 gallons of water.

My thinking was that because a swimming pool has a finite amount of water, it would be possible to locate the lens. I set off with a small fishnet and spent thirty minutes swimming around like a blue whale sifting out krill. Believe it or not, I found the lens—though not by using a fishnet.

Instead, I checked the pool filter the next day, and there was the lens. I didn't think it was wise to use that lens again after it had been soaking in chlorinated water for a day, but still, I did find it.

Wisdom

- Believe in the unbelievable. I found a contact lens in a swimming pool! What are the odds of that? Talk about giving hope to the hopeless.

- Use the right tool. I found the lens because thousands of gallons of water went through the pool filter, not because I swam around with a fishing net like an idiot.

Quitters Can Win

If you were an Asian American (or Jewish) kid in the 1970s, your parents wanted you to become a dentist, doctor, or lawyer. After the fainting episode at Stanford Medical Center, medicine was out for me. I didn't want to spend my life sticking my hands in people's mouths, so dentistry was out as well.

Only law was left. This career choice made sense because my father, who didn't finish college, enacted laws as a state senator in Hawaii. He wanted me to get a law degree—each generation making progress and all. I applied to law school at Stanford, UC Berkeley, and UC Davis, and I got in to UC Davis.

In the fall of 1976, I entered law school. Davis is a small city near Sacramento. In 1980, it had a population of 36,000 people, which was even lower when I was there. The school is best known for its agriculture and veterinary curriculum.

If his goal was to intimidate us, he was too effective on me.

A classmate from 'Iolani named Russell Kato had been accepted at the same time, and we shared an apartment. During orientation week, one of the deans told us that although we were bright, we didn't know shit, and law school was going to remake our brains.

If his goal was to intimidate us, he was too effective on me. The law school case-study method involved the professor's calling on students and ripping them to pieces. (Remember how the Harvard Law School professor played by John Houseman humiliates his students in the movie *The Paper Chase?*)

So, for the second time in my life, I quit something (quitting the Stanford football team was the first). I didn't even finish the orientation program. I regret leaving Russell Kato high and dry without a roommate. I also felt that I had failed my parents, because they had

Russell Kato and me, thirty-seven years later.

worked so hard and sacrificed so much so I could attend college and law school.

I feared that they would be furious—perhaps even disown me—when I told them of my decision. But to my surprise, my father said, "It's okay . . . as long as you make something of yourself by the time you're twenty-five or so. Just don't waste your life."

I never felt closer to my father than at that moment. Four decades later, my assessment of quitting law school is that it proved my self-awareness; many people practice law for twenty years before they figure out they're miserable. I came to the same conclusion in only a week.

Don't fear the impact of quitting something. People are reluctant to quit for these reasons:

- They'll slide down a slippery slope and become perennial quitters.
- Quitting will make them look stupid or weak, because winners are always smart and strong.
- They will let down their parents, friends, teachers, and coaches.

Quitting something doesn't necessarily make you a perennial quitter, or stupid, or weak. It's just one instance and one decision. Granted, if you make quitting a habit, you have a problem.

What you do *after* you quit is more important than the fact that you quit. Do you reboot, remake, and restart, or do you give up? This is what determines whether you disappoint others and yourself as well.

Old People Rule

In June 1995, I stood in front of the graduating class of Palo Alto High School and delivered a baccalaureate speech. Over the course of my career, I've given similar speeches at the Harker School, De Anza College, Menlo College, High Tech High of San Diego, Woodside Priory, Babson College, and UCLA Anderson School of Management.

Since the topic of this chapter is inspiration, I'm including the text of the speech in the hope that it will inspire you. Over the years, many people have told me that it motivated them.

Commencement speech at Menlo College, 2012.

Speaking to you today marks a milestone in my life. I am forty years old. Twenty-two years ago, when I was in your seat, I never, ever thought I would be forty years old.

The implications of being your speaker frightens me. For one thing, when a forty-year-old geezer spoke at my baccalaureate ceremony, he was about the last person I'd believe.

I have no intention of giving you the boring speech that you are dreading. This speech will be short, sweet, and not boring. I am going to talk about hindsights today. Hindsights that I've accumulated in the twenty years from where you are to where I am.

Don't blindly believe me. Don't take what I say as "truth." Just listen. Perhaps my experiences can help you out a tiny bit. I will present them à la David Letterman. Yes, forty-year-old people can still stay up past 11:00 p.m.

#10: Live off your parents as long as possible.

When I spoke at this ceremony two years ago, this was the most popular hindsight—except from the point of view of the parents. Thus, I knew I was on the right track.

I was a diligent Oriental in high school and college. I took college-level classes and earned college-level credits. I rushed through college in three and a half years. I never traveled or took time off because I thought it wouldn't prepare me for work and it would delay my graduation.

Frankly, I blew it.

You are going to work the rest of your lives, so don't be in a rush to start. Stretch out your college education. Now is the time to suck life into your lungs, before you have a mortgage, kids, and car payments. Take whole semesters off to travel over-seas. Take jobs and internships that pay less money or no money. Investigate your passions on your parents' nickel. Or dime. Or quarter. Or dollar.

Your goal should be to extend college to at least six years. Delay, as long as possible, the inevitable entry into the work-place and a lifetime of servitude to bozos who know less than you do but make more money. Also, you shouldn't deprive your parents of the pleasure of supporting you.

#9: Pursue joy, not happiness.

This is probably the hardest lesson of all to learn. It probably seems that the goal in life is to be "happy." Oh, you may have to sacrifice and study and work hard, but, by and large, happiness should be predictable. Nice house. Nice car. Nice material things.

Take my word for it: happiness is temporary and fleeting. Joy, by contrast, is unpredictable. It comes from pursuing interests and passions that do not obviously result in happiness. Pursuing joy, not happiness, will translate into one thing over the next few years for you. Study what you love. This may also not be popular with parents.

When I went to college, I was "market driven." It's also an Oriental thing. I looked at what fields had the greatest job opportunities and prepared myself for them. This was brain-dead. There are so many ways to make a living in the world; it doesn't matter that you've taken all the "right" courses.

I don't think one person on the original Macintosh team had a classic "computer science" degree. You parents have a responsibility in this area. Don't force your kids to follow in your footsteps or to live your dreams. My father was a senator in Hawaii. His dream was to be a lawyer, but he only had a high school education. He wanted me to be a lawyer.

For him, I went to law school. For me, I quit after a week. I view this as a validation of my inherent intelligence.

#8: Challenge the known and embrace the unknown.

One of the biggest mistakes you can make in life is to accept the known and resist the unknown. You should, in fact, do exactly the opposite: challenge the known and embrace the unknown.

Let me tell you a short story about ice. In the late 1800s, there was a thriving ice-harvesting industry in the Northeast. Companies would cut blocks of ice from frozen lakes and ponds and sell them around the world. The largest single shipment was two hundred tons, which was shipped to India. One hundred tons got there before melting, but this was enough to make a profit.

The ice harvesters, however, were put out of business by companies that invented mechanical ice makers. It was no longer necessary to cut and ship ice because companies could make it in any city during any season.

The ice makers, however, were put out of business by refrigerator companies. If it was convenient to make ice at a manufacturing plant, imagine how much better it was to make ice and create cold storage in everyone's home.

You would think that the ice harvesters would see the advantages of ice factories and adopt this technology. However, all they could think about was the known: better saws, better storage, better transportation. Then you would think that the ice makers would see the advantages of refrigerators and adopt this technology.

The truth is that the ice harvesters couldn't embrace the unknown and jump from their curve to the next curve. Challenge the known and embrace the unknown, or you'll be like the ice harvesters and ice factories.

#7: Learn to speak a foreign language, play a musical instrument, and play non-contact sports.

I studied Latin in high school because I thought it would help me increase my vocabulary. It did, but trust me when I tell you it's very difficult to have a conversation in Latin today, other than at the Vatican. And despite all my efforts, the pope has yet to call for my advice.

Learn to play a musical instrument. My only connection to music today is that I was named after Guy Lombardo. Trust me: it's better than being named after Guy's brother Carmen. Playing a musical instrument could be with me now and stay with me forever. Instead, I have to buy CDs at Tower.

I played football. I loved football. Football is macho. I was a middle linebacker—arguably one of the most macho positions in a macho game. But you should also learn to play a non-contact sport like basketball or tennis. That is, a sport you can play when you're over the hill.

It will be as difficult when you're forty to get twenty-two guys together in a stadium to play football as it is to have a conversation in Latin, but all the people who wore cute white tennis outfits can still play tennis. And all the macho football players are sitting around watching television and drinking beer.

#6: Continue to learn.

Learning is a process, not an event. I thought learning would be over when I got my degree. It's not true. You should never stop learning.

Indeed, it gets easier to learn once you're out of school because it's easier to see the relevance of why you need to learn. You're learning in a structured, dedicated environment right now. On your parents' nickel.

But don't confuse school and learning. You can go to school and not learn a thing. You can also learn a tremendous amount without school.

#5: Learn to like yourself, or change yourself until you can like yourself.

I know a forty-year-old woman who was a drug addict. She is a mother of three. She traced the start of her drug addiction to smoking dope in high school.

I'm not going to lecture you about not taking drugs. Hey, I smoked dope in high school. Unlike Bill Clinton, I inhaled. Also unlike Bill Clinton, I exhaled.

This woman told me that she started taking drugs because she hated herself when she was sober. She did not like drugs as much as she hated herself. Drugs were not the problem, though she thought they were the solution.

She turned her life around only after she realized that she was in a downward spiral. Fix your problem. Fix your life. Then you won't need to take drugs. Drugs are neither the solution nor the problem. Frankly, smoking, drugs, alcohol, and using an IBM PC are signs of stupidity. End of discussion.

#4: Don't get married too soon.

I got married when I was thirty-two. That's about the right age. Until you're about that age, you may not know who you are. You also may not know whom you're marrying. I don't know one person who got married too late. I know many people who got married too young. If you decide to get married, just keep in mind that you need to accept the person for what he or she is right now.

#3: Play to win and win to play.

Playing to win is one of the finest things you can do. It enables you to fulfill your potential. It enables you to improve the world and, conveniently, develop high expectations for everyone else, too.

And what if you lose? Just make sure you lose while trying something grand. Avinash Dixit, an economics professor at Princeton, and Barry Nalebuff, an economics and management professor at the Yale School of Organization and Management, say it this way: "If you are going to fail, you might as well fail at a difficult task. Failure causes others to downgrade their expectations of you in the future. The seriousness of this problem depends on what you attempt."

In its purest form, winning becomes a means, not an end, to improve yourself and your competition. Winning is also a means to play again. The unexamined life may not be worth living, but the unlived life is not worth examining.

The rewards of winning—money, power, satisfaction, and self-confidence—should not be squandered. Thus, in addition to playing to win, you have a second, more important obligation: to compete again to the depth and breadth and height that your soul can reach. Ultimately, your greatest competition is your own self.

#2: Obey the absolutes.

Playing to win, however, does not mean playing dirty. As you grow older and older, you will find that things change from absolute to relative. When you were very young, it was absolutely wrong to lie, cheat, or steal. As you get older, and particularly when you enter the workforce, you will be tempted by the "system" to think in relative terms.

"I made more money." "I have a nicer car." "I went on a better vacation." Worse, "I didn't cheat as much on my taxes as my partner." "I just have a few drinks. I don't take cocaine." "I don't pad my expense reports as much as others."

This is completely wrong. Preserve and obey the absolutes as much as you can. If you never lie, cheat, or steal, you will never have to remember who you lied to, how you cheated, and what you stole. There absolutely are absolute rights and wrongs.

#1: Enjoy your family and friends before they are gone.

This is the most important hindsight. It doesn't require much explanation. I'll just repeat it: enjoy your family and friends before they are gone. Nothing—not money, power, or fame—can replace your family and friends or bring them back once they are gone.

Our greatest joy has been our baby, and I predict that

children will bring you the greatest joy in your lives—especially if they graduate from college in four years.

And now I'm going to give you one extra hindsight, because I've probably cost your parents thousands of dollars today. It's something that I hate to admit, too. By and large, the older you get, the more you're going to realize that your parents were right. More and more—until finally, you become your parents.

I know you're all saying, "Yeah, right." Mark my words.

Remember these eleven things: if just one of them helps just one of you, this speech will have been a success:

#10: Live off your parents as long as possible.

#9: Pursue joy, not happiness.

#8: Challenge the known and embrace the unknown.

#7: Learn to speak a foreign language, play a musical instrument, and play non-contact sports.

#6: Continue to learn.

#5: Learn to like yourself, or change yourself until you can like yourself.

#4: Don't get married too soon.

#3: Play to win and win to play.

#2: Obey the absolutes.

#1: Enjoy your family and friends before they are gone.

Bonus: You're going to become your parents.

Congratulations on your graduation. Thank you very much.

04

Apple

You've baked a really lovely cake,
but then you've used dog shit for frosting.

—Steve Jobs

I worked at Apple from 1983 to 1987, and then from 1995 to 1997. Although I refer to these stints as "two tours of duty," it was a privilege and an honor to work there. In many ways, I am who I am and where I am because of Steve Jobs and Apple.

Just Get In

Most companies rely on educational background and work experience to determine the acceptability of job candidates. The logic is that employees need a foundation of relevant knowledge and skills to succeed—or at least not make the hiring manager look bad.

But this wasn't how I got my job at Apple. I joined the company in September 1983. On paper (this was before LinkedIn), my résumé should not have gotten me an interview. My educational background was a bachelor of arts in psychology and a master of business administration in marketing. I had not taken a computer class—not that there were many computer classes back then.

My work experience was also seemingly irrelevant. After earning my MBA, I went to work for a fine jewelry manufacturer. I started out by counting diamonds and left five years later as vice president of sales and marketing. My only exposure to computers was using an IBM System/32 to enter and access data.

While I was in the jewelry business, my Stanford classmate Mike Boich introduced me to an Apple II, and I fell in love with word processors, spreadsheets, and databases. Word processing, in particular,

The first three generations of Macintosh evangelists: Mike Boich, me, and Alain Rossmann. Mike started Macintosh evangelism, Alain Rossmann did the work, and I took the credit.

was a godsend that was much better than the state-of-the-art IBM Selectric typewriter featuring sticky tape to lift off mistakes. Give me AppleWorks, QuickFile, and VisiCalc, and I was ready for anything.

My love of computers inspired me to get a job in the industry, and in early 1983 Mike told me there was a position in the Macintosh Division to run the Apple University Consortium. This was a program to sell Macs to prestigious universities in order to get their students to use them.

The Macintosh Division's thinking was that the students would become Mac users for the rest of their lives and also evangelize Macintosh at the companies they worked for after graduation. We had seen similar long-term effects when kids used Apple IIs in elementary through high school.

As part of the hiring process, Boich took me into the Macintosh Division building on Bandley Drive in Cupertino and demonstrated MacWrite and MacPaint. When he did, the clouds parted, angels started singing, and I was dumbfounded by how cool Macintosh was.

> . . . the clouds parted, angels started singing, and I was dumbfounded by how cool Macintosh was.

The Apple University Consortium job was given to someone else, but I was determined to get into the computer industry after the religious experience of seeing a Mac. I applied to a dozen computer companies, and I was rejected by each one because I had neither a technical degree nor computer work experience.

My break came in 1982 at COMDEX, a computer industry show, in Las Vegas. There I stumbled across a company called Edu-Ware Services, an educational software publishing company in Agoura Hills,

The Macintosh Division, circa 1984. This is the only known
instance of Steve Jobs getting on his knees for anyone.

California. The person running its sales and marketing, Mike Lieberman, had been injured in a car accident on the way to the show, so there was an opening for which I was hired.

In July 1983, Management Science America of Atlanta, Georgia, bought Edu-Ware and placed the company in the Peachtree software division. The folks at Peachtree tried to convince me to move to Atlanta, but I declined because I couldn't live in a place where sushi was called "bait" and every street was named Peachtree.

Fortunately, Boich contacted me with another opening in the Macintosh Division as a "software evangelist." That position involved convincing software and hardware companies to create Macintosh products. I got the job through nepotism—the practice of people giving jobs to their friends and relatives—not because of my work or educational background.

The Macintosh Division, circa 2009.

My entry into the organization was inauspicious, because Steve Jobs's ringing endorsement was that he liked me, but he wasn't blown away. His words were, as Boich told me decades later, "You can hire Guy, but you're betting your job on him."

To be fair, a psych major with an MBA in marketing who had schlepped gold and diamonds wasn't the ideal candidate for the position, but evangelizing Macintosh to developers was fundamentally sales. And sales, because of my jewelry background, was something I could do.

For the first six months, I carried Mike's bags as we visited software developers around the country. Eventually I took over his role and hit the road to convince companies to bet on a computer with no installed base, half-done tools, and draft documentation.

Luckily for Boich, I succeeded at Apple, and Jobs never fired either of us. I thrived at Apple for these reasons:

- Macintosh was a great product. Between you and me, any moderately capable person could have succeeded at my job, because Macintosh was so innovative.
- I was in the right place at the right time. Personal computers were just taking off in the mid-1980s, and there I was. Sometimes it's better to be lucky than smart.
- Evangelizing Macintosh involved hand-to-hand sales. The process wasn't about A/B testing of the colors on a home page or prospecting through "big data." The jewelry business prepared me well for this kind of old-fashioned selling.
- I loved to work. There are people who are smarter than me. There are people who work harder than me. But there are few people who are both. My ability to grind out work is the reason I succeeded in the Macintosh Division and, really, in life.

Wisdom

Don't worry about the "minimum requirements" of a job. They represent wishful thinking rather than nonnegotiable prerequisites. Few, if any, candidates embody them all.

Your task is to make the person doing the hiring forget about the "requirements" because you are so strong in other areas. There are no perfect candidates—there are only successful candidates who made their shortcomings irrelevant.

Get in any way you can. Don't be proud. The day after you start a job, nobody cares about your connections, history, and credentials—or lack thereof. You either deliver results, or you don't.

> Get in at any level you can. The rising tide floats all boats. The level you rise to is what's important, not the level at which you entered. So take that internship, software tester, database administrator, or receptionist job and build from there.

> Learn to disregard two factors when you're doing the hiring: (1) the lack of a perfect education and perfect work experience of a candidate who loves the product; and (2) the presence of a perfect education and perfect work experience of a candidate who doesn't love the product.

The day after you start a job, nobody cares about your connections, history, and credentials—or lack thereof.

The Truth Works

One day sometime in 1984, Jobs appeared in my cubicle with a man I didn't know. He didn't introduce him—Jobs wasn't long on social niceties. Instead, he asked, "What do you think of a company called Knoware?"

I told Jobs that the company's products were mediocre, boring, and simplistic and that the company was not strategic for us. After all, they didn't take advantage of the Mac graphical user interface and other advanced features.

After my diatribe, Jobs said to me, "I want you to meet the CEO of Knoware, Archie McGill." I shook his hand, and Steve said to him, "See? That's what I told you."

Thank you, Steve.

In the Macintosh Division, you had to prove yourself every day, or Jobs got rid of you. He demanded excellence and kept you at the top of your game. It wasn't easy to work for him; it was sometimes unpleasant and always scary, but it drove many of us to do the finest work of our careers.

I wouldn't trade working for him for any job I've ever had—and I don't know anyone in the Macintosh Division who would.

Wisdom

Tell the truth. Honesty is a test of your competence and character. You need intelligence to recognize what is true, and you need strength to speak it.

The wiser the person, the more they yearn for the truth. Telling people that their product is good in order to be kind or positive doesn't help them improve it—much less impress or fool people like Jobs.

Honesty is not only better, it's also easier than lying. There's only one truth, so being consistent is simple if you're honest. If you are not honest, you have to concoct a lie and then keep track of what you said.

If I had said nice things about the crappy Knoware products, Jobs would have, at a minimum, decided that I was clueless, and that would have limited my career at Apple. At worst, he would have said that I was shit and fired me later that day, if not on the spot.

What's $745,000 Between Friends?

In 1986, Apple had a problem: we were running out of "fans" who would buy anything from the company they loved. Unfortunately, other people weren't buying Macs because they thought there wasn't a large enough selection of software. (They were right, but we didn't let the truth get in the way of Macintosh evangelism.)

Mike Murray, the Macintosh Division's director of marketing, told me to change this perception of reality. We decided that Apple's dealers and Apple's salespeople were the right place to start to change this impression, so we had to convince them that Macintosh had lots of innovative software.

We came up with a plan to buy 1,500 copies of ten different software programs at $50 each to give them. Murray told me to execute the plan, so I contacted the ten companies and negotiated the deal. Back then software cost $200 to $500, so a $50 price was a huge discount. However, because this program offered exposure to Apple's dealers and salesforce, the companies quickly agreed.

So far, so good. Everything rolled along, and while the software companies built the inventory, I got a purchase order for $750,000 (1,500 copies x 10 programs x $50/copy). I presented the invoices to the finance department, and Susan Barnes, the vice president of finance for the Macintosh Division, went berserk. My spending limit was $5,000, so she was incensed that I had spent a mere $745,000 more than that.

Rumor had it that Jobs told her to fire me. My side of the story was

> She said Steve had had no intention of firing me—he just wanted her to scare the shit out of me.

that Murray, my boss, had told me to get it done, so I got it done. Fast-forward to 2016. At a reunion of Macintosh Division employees, I asked Barnes about this story. She said Steve had had no intention of firing me—he just wanted her to scare the shit out of me.

I still believe that I did the right thing. If you tell some people to get something done, they will do it. Murray told me to change the perception that Macintosh lacked software, and he also told me that we had the budget, so I did what I had to do. End of story.

Wisdom

Trust, but document—especially if you've spent 150 times your expense limit! It's good to cover your ass when you're bending the rules. I should have sent Murray a memo confirming that he wanted me to buy the software. Then he would have had to deal with the wrath of Jobs, not me.

The Art of Bluffing

During my first tour of duty at Apple, I had the privilege of working with Jack Brown of the law firm Brown and Bain. He and his firm represented Apple in the intellectual property lawsuits against Digital Research and Microsoft in the 1980s.

Apple sued Digital Research because it had created an operating system called GEM (graphical environment manager) that, at least according to us, ripped off the Macintosh graphical user interface. At the beginning of the lawsuit, Jack Brown, his team, and several of us from Apple went to Digital Research's office in Monterey to confront the company.

I drove down with Brown. For much of the trip, he told me how weak our case was because Xerox's Palo Alto Research Center had created a similar user interface before Apple. Also, according to Brown, "A window is a window, and a trash can is a trash can. You can't own such simple concepts." I got out of the car thinking our lawsuit was doomed.

Then the meeting began, and he started with a ten-minute sermon about the immoral, heinous, and unconscionable crime Digital Research had committed. I'm paraphrasing, but he went on the attack: "In my entire career I've never seen a more blatant transgression of intellectual property," and "I don't know why we're meeting. We should go straight to court."

These accusations flew through the air like tracer bullets from an A-10 Warthog. Less than an hour before, he had told me we had no chance of winning. Now I was hearing that intellectual property law as well as the universe's moral compass were on our side. It was motherhood, apple pie, and the Macintosh user interface.

Wisdom

"Anchor" people. This means that you communicate a large claim or monetary amount if you're selling or a small claim or monetary amount if you're buying.

For example, when Brown (the "seller") postulated that copying the Mac user interface was a heinous crime, it would have been difficult for Digital Research to counter that it was a minor mistake or transgression.

If Digital Research (the "buyer") had spoken first, then it could have tried to anchor us by claiming what it did was a minor mistake or transgression. Then it would take a master litigator/negotiator to still insist it was a heinous crime—which Brown was, so it wouldn't have worked.

 Don't be anchored. Assume that your adversary is trying to anchor you, and don't play the game by those rules. Put your own claim or number out there as if you didn't hear anything.

As the saying goes, "Fake it until you litigate it." That day, Jack Brown made me a better negotiator for the rest of my life.

The Time I Almost Quit Apple

In 1986, I was up for a promotion at Apple. The next level was a directorship—which meant a raise, more stock options, and a company car.

My boss was the chief operating officer of Apple, Del Yocam. In my review he told me that the young, small-development businesses loved me. This included companies like Silicon Beach Software, Telos, and T/Maker—places that you probably never heard of.

That was the good news.

The bad news was that three businesses *didn't* like me: Microsoft, Lotus Development Corporation, and Ashton-Tate. I was pleased that he knew this, because they were companies that shouldn't have liked me because:

- Microsoft ripped off the Mac user interface.
- Lotus created a piece of crap called Jazz.
- Ashton-Tate also created a piece of crap called dBASE Mac.

The review was going so well that I contemplated how big my raise would be and what kind of car to get, but Del didn't see it that way. He thought those three companies were critical for Apple, so I didn't get the promotion.

I was dumbfounded. The enemy of your enemy is your friend, and the friend of your enemy is your enemy, but isn't your enemy your enemy? I was so pissed off that I almost resigned the next day.

I was so pissed off that I almost resigned the next day.

Wisdom

Communicate with your boss so you know what achievements she's looking for. The rules of the game and the way the score is kept should not surprise you.

Woe unto me, because I should have known that Del Yocam wanted me to make the big developers, including Microsoft, Lotus, and Ashton-Tate, happy, too. If you think about it, there's no way his perspective could have been, "Make the small developers happy and piss off the big ones."

This debacle was my fault, too, and I should have known better than to assume that making small developers happy was enough.

The Time I Did Quit Apple

Within a day of my disappointing meeting with Del Yocam, I saw Jean-Louis Gassée, another executive who reported to Yocam. I told him I was pissed off and about to quit.

Gassée explained that Apple was reorganizing the management structure, and he would soon be my boss. He went on to say that being a director at Apple was excellent for my résumé, so I should stay another six months, and he would promote me to director at my next review.

True to his word, he did. However, I resigned on April 1, 1987, the day after my promotion, in order to start a software company called ACIUS with a remarkable Frenchwoman named Marylene Delbourg-Delphis, a programmer named Laurent Ribardière, and a product manager named Will Mayall (who became my best friend for life).

At the time, Apple was still fighting the perception that Macintosh lacked software. Rather than solely depending on external developers, it had decided to publish on its own a handful of products such as MacWrite, MacPaint, MacDraw, and 4th Dimension.

Ashton-Tate's dBASE, a relational database, was a killer app for the IBM PC. The thinking was that if Mac was going to succeed as a business computer, it needed a good relational database. Ashton-Tate didn't believe in Macintosh enough to make a good database for Macintosh.

Meanwhile, Ribardière and Delbourg-Delphis had created 4th Dimension in Paris, and it was a great product, so Apple acquired the publishing rights to it with the intent of making it an Apple-labeled product. When Ashton-Tate found out about Apple's competitive product, the company's CEO went straight to the top and complained to John Sculley, then CEO of Apple, and Yocam. Sculley and Yocam caved in and gave 4th Dimension back to Ribardière and Delbourg-Delphis.

There was good synergy between Ribardière, Delbourg-Delphis, and me because we all were pissed off with Apple, and we all thought 4th Dimension was a killer product. So we decided to start a company called ACIUS to publish it. I re-signed from Apple and became the CEO. The company still exists today.

Another thing happened at ACIUS that changed my life: I wrote my first book, *The Macintosh Way*. Without Delbourg-Delphis's encouragement and faith, I would not have written that book. She has provided great support for several of my other books as well.

> ## Without Delbourg-Delphis's encouragement and faith, I would not have written that book.

Wisdom

Quit a job when the timing is optimal. Gassée was right: having an Apple directorship on my résumé was useful for my career because "software evangelist" and, later, "software product manager" did not have the gravitas of "director."

Don't quit because of reactionary emotions such as anger and disappointment. Plan your exit. Try to have the next job or opportunity in place. The timing and manner of quitting a job are just as important as the timing and manner of starting a job.

People Who Love Your Product Are a Powerful Force

My second tour of duty at Apple started in 1995. At the time, my wife, Beth, and I were living in San Francisco with our first son, and she was in beta with our second child. I was pursuing my bliss as a writer, speaker, and consultant when Dan Eilers, a vice president at Apple, reached out to me.

If you can believe it, many people thought then that Apple was going to die. Steve Jobs would not make his triumphant return for another two years. Macintosh was a mediocre success, and there were layoffs, executive turmoil, and a tarnishing of the brand.

Eilers asked me to return to Apple as an Apple fellow and chief evangelist. My job was to preserve the Macintosh cult, and because I loved Apple, I answered the call.

I worked with Mac user groups, developers, and anyone with a pulse who still believed in the product and the company. The most powerful tool I had was EvangeList, an opt-in email list that broadcast positive

Guy Kawasaki
Chief Evangelist

Apple Computer, Inc.
One Infinite Loop, MS: 303-4GK
Cupertino, California 95014
408 974-2359 Fax: 408 257-4618
Email: Kawasaki@apple.com

My Apple business card.

news about Apple and Macintosh and new-product announcements from developers.

It had more than forty thousand subscribers. This sounds puny relative to sites such as Facebook and Twitter today, but an army of forty thousand true believers was a big deal back then (and might still be). EvangeList was a key factor in Apple's survival because it kept Mac believers going when most people were pessimistic about Apple's chances.

By far the biggest cause of Apple's rebound and success was the return of Steve Jobs. The first thing he did was to pare down the Macintosh product line and then add the line of colorful, all-in-one Macs called iMac. (Only Steve could convince the world that repackaging a computer in bright colors was revolutionary.)

However, the preservation of the Macintosh cult and developer community was also important, because it's lonely at the bottom. These folks continued to buy Macs, convince others to buy Macs, and develop Mac software and hardware. The revenue from Macintosh enabled Apple to create the iPod, and in 2017 Apple became the most valuable publicly traded company of all time.

Wisdom

Embrace people who want to help. People love to contribute to a cause they believe in. You don't need to pay them—indeed, *don't* pay them, because they don't want to feel like they were "bought."

But you do need to ask for their help and then make them feel that they are part of the team. The survival and success of Apple prove that you should never underestimate the value of customers who love what you do.

> I also learned that the foundation of evangelism is a great product. This phenomenon is "Guy's Golden Touch"—not that whatever I touched turned to gold, but whatever was gold, I touched. It's easy to get people excited about a great product; it's hard to get people excited about crap.

The Time I Quit Again

Near the end of my second tour of duty at Apple, Jobs sold NeXT to Apple and became an advisor to the company. The last meeting I attended with Jobs was a gathering of the marketing team and Lee Clow from Apple's advertising agency, Chiat/Day. Lee showed us the "Think Different" campaign for the first time, and to put it mildly, we loved it.

"That's okay, Steve. I don't trust you, either."

At the end of the meeting, Clow said he had two copies of the video of the ads, and he would give one to Jobs and one to me. In front of everyone, Jobs told Clow not to give me a copy.

I don't know what got into my brain, but I said, "Why, Steve, don't you trust me?" And Steve responded, "No, I don't."

And I countered, "That's okay, Steve. I don't trust you, either." That response may have cost me tens of millions of dollars, because I clearly burned a bridge for working at Apple when Jobs returned.

I left Apple shortly thereafter. At the time, there was a constant flow of stories of how executives were abandoning ship. I didn't want to add to this body of evidence of gloom and doom. Instead, I went on a leave of absence, Apple made no announcement (no one announces a leave of absence), and I never returned.

There wasn't any press coverage about my leaving. It might have been gratifying if there had been, but it was better for Apple and for me that I slipped out in the dark of night. Whatever attention my departure would garner would last a few days, but Google searches would have forever associated my name with results like "Key Executive Abandons Apple."

A few years later I saw Jobs at a tech conference, and he asked me to return to run Apple University, the internal training curriculum for Apple employees. I turned that down, too. That probably cost me another few tens of millions of dollars.

Now you know that you're reading the book of someone who quit Apple twice and turned down a job offer to return for a third stint. I hope you don't regret it.

Wisdom

Be careful about leaving a company too early. What's worse: leaving too early or staying too long? I'd say leaving too early.

The grass is not always greener. And brown grass can turn green. There are two broad career paths:

- Stay put and grind it out with the same company.
- Move on to a new opportunity.

Both can work. Both can fail. If I could tell you which path to pick to guarantee success, this book would cost much more than you paid. The popular theory is to constantly change jobs, but my Apple experience contradicts this.

I didn't know, and couldn't have known, that Apple would become as successful as it did. I'm not alone—most of the Macintosh Division left Apple "too early." People who say they "knew" Apple would become the most valuable company in the world are bullshitting. No one knew, not even Jobs.

On the other hand, if I had stayed at Apple, my life would have been less interesting. I wouldn't have started companies, become a venture capitalist, advised dozens of entrepreneurs, spoken at hundreds of events all over the world, and written fifteen books.

There's More to a Job Than Money and Perks

Speaking of staying put, in 2010, I asked a longtime Apple employee why he remained at the company. By that time, it was difficult for most employees to make millions of dollars on Apple stock because there were tens of thousands of employees and the company already had a high market valuation. Plus, working for a company run by a domineering person like Jobs wasn't easy.

The employee's answer stunned me: "I stay at Apple because it enables me to do the best work of my career. Every company has bullshit, but at least at Apple, I know that the person at the top knows when I do good work."

So true. Unlike Jobs, the top management of most tech companies cannot judge whether products are good. They throw around words like "revolutionary," "innovative," and "disruptive," but they really don't know good stuff when they see it, and they certainly have difficulty inspiring good stuff.

That is one reason there are so many mediocre and ugly products—
and why Jobs and Apple crushed the competition for several decades.

Wisdom

Don't assume that the only motivational tools for employee
recruitment and retention are money and fringe benefits.
There are always organizations that can pay more or provide
better perks.

However, the opportunity to learn new skills, operate inde-
pendently, contribute to a higher purpose, and work for people
who have the smarts to know when you've done good work is
rare and valuable.

Daniel Pink explains this concept magnificently in his book
Drive: The Surprising Truth About What Motivates Us. (You
should read it.) His acronym is MAP: Mastery, Autonomy, and
Purpose.

If you're an employee, look beyond salary and perks. Does
the job enable you to master new skills while working autonomously toward a meaningful goal?

If you're a boss, are you offering employees a way to master
new skills while working autonomously toward a meaningful goal?

Agreement Breaks Down Walls

From 1984 to 1987, Apple tried to position Mac as a word-processing,
database, and spreadsheet machine. We went zero for three during that
period, because companies did not embrace the Mac as a viable replace-
ment for the IBM PC for these business applications.

Fortunately, Paul Brainerd and the team at Aldus Corporation created PageMaker, and John Warnock and the team at Adobe created PostScript. PageMaker was a desktop publishing application that enabled Mac users to create books, newspapers, newsletters, and magazines. PostScript was the technology that powered Apple's laser printers and democratized beautiful printing.

Soon, businesses of all sizes embraced the Mac as a desktop publishing machine, and sales took off. This was the first time the market and Apple were in agreement that the Mac was a desirable personal computer. It's not an exaggeration to say that desktop publishing saved Apple.

"Guy-ah"—he made my name two syllables—"I was born too late for slaves and too early for robots."

During that time, one of my favorite duties at Apple was supporting Macintosh user groups. This wasn't in my job description—I volunteered to help these hardy souls because they believed in Mac so much. Some of my fondest memories from my Apple days are from user group experiences.

Once on a visit to Mobile, Alabama, to speak to a Mac user group, I had a most awkward and entertaining experience. At a reception after the meeting, a member of the group told me in his Southern drawl, "Guy-ah"—he made my name two syllables—"I was born too late for slaves and too early for robots."

At the time, I wondered how he could say this to me, a member of a racial minority. Was he blind? Did he think slavery was okay? Did he really wish he'd been born earlier so he could own slaves?

I finally figured out that our common passion for Macintosh trumped our different racial backgrounds and philosophy of personal freedom.

The Gospel According to Steve

My two tours of duty at Apple were remarkable experiences that defined my career. To conclude this chapter, here is a list of the top eleven lessons I learned at Apple:

1. *Only excellence matters.* Steve Jobs elevated women to positions of power long before it was cool or socially responsible to do so. He didn't care about gender, sexual orientation, race, creed, or color. He divided the world into two groups: insanely great people and crappy people. It was that simple.

Panel of Steve's direct reports. He was way ahead of his time.

2. *Customers can't tell you what they need.* In the early 1980s, Apple was selling Apple IIs. If you asked customers what they wanted, they would say a bigger, faster, and cheaper Apple II. No one would have asked for a Mac.

3. *Innovation happens on the next curve.* Macintosh was the next curve in personal computing. It wasn't merely an improvement to the Apple II or MS-DOS curve. Innovation isn't making a slightly better status quo. It's about jumping to the next curve.

4. *Design counts.* It may not count for everyone, but design counts for many people. Steve was obsessed with great design. He drove us nuts with his attention to detail, but that is what made Apple successful.

5. *Less is more.* One of the key tenets of Steve's obsession with design was the belief that less is more. He was the minimalist's minimalist. You can even see this in his slides: they had dark blue or black backgrounds

with large white text and no more than a handful of words.

6. *Big challenges beget big accomplishments.* The goal of the Macintosh Division was preventing totalitarianism and worldwide domination by IBM. Merely shipping yet another computer was never the goal.

7. *Changing your mind is a sign of intelligence.* When Steve announced the iPhone, he stated that it was a closed-programming system to ensure that it was safe and reliable. A year later, he opened it up to apps, and iPhone sales skyrocketed. This was a 180-degree reversal and a sign of intelligence, because a closed-programming iPhone was a mistake.

8. *Engineers are artists.* Steve treated engineers like artists. They weren't cogs in a machine whose output was measured in lines of code. Macintosh was an artistic expression by engineers whose palette was software and hardware design.

9. *Price and value are not the same thing.* No one ever bought a Mac based on price. Its true value became evident only when you factored in the lower requirements for support and training. Steve seldom fought on price, but he won wars because of value.

10. *But value isn't enough.* Many products are valuable, but if your product isn't also unique or differentiated in some way, you have to compete on price. You can succeed this way—as Dell did, for example. But if you truly want to "dent the universe," your product needs to be both unique and valuable.

11. *Some things need to be believed to be seen.* Innovators ignore naysayers to get the job done. The "experts" told Steve he was wrong many times: Macintosh, iPod, iPhone, and Apple retail stores, for example. It's not that Steve was always right, but sometimes you need to believe in something in order to see it.

05

Business

The successful warrior is the average man,
with laser-like focus.

—Bruce Lee

I learned business lessons as a sales guy for a jewelry manufacturer, evangelist for Apple, high-tech CEO several times over, venture capitalist, chief evangelist for Canva, and brand ambassador for Mercedes-Benz. I made many mistakes in these positions, and I discuss them here so you can at least make *different* mistakes.

Selling Is a Crucial Skill

When I dropped out of law school, I wasn't done with formal education. In the fall of 1977, I entered the MBA program at UCLA.

Northwestern had also accepted me, but I looked at the subzero winters of Illinois and passed the IQ test by picking Southern California—further confirmation of my nascent intelligence.

UCLA, Santa Monica, and the MBA program were a much better fit than law school. I loved the whole concept of running a business and making money. I even liked finance, statistics, and operations research.

The UCLA MBA program had four days of classes per week. Friday was a day to gain real-world experience—or goof off. During the first year of my MBA program, I met a woman from Hawaii named Lynn Nakamura. She was a dynamo who worked for a jewelry manufacturer called Nova Stylings. This company was owned by the Gruber family, and it sold jewelry to retailers including Tiffany, Cartier, Tivol, Mayors, and Zales.

Lynn ran the diamond department. That meant she sorted the diamonds by size and quality and picked them for the diamond setters. She offered me a part-time job counting diamonds and helping in the shipping and receiving department. With a four-day week, I had plenty of time for a part-time job, and I needed spending money.

As a result, my life took an unpredictable turn, since "jeweler" was not one of the preferred career paths for Asian Americans. When I graduated from UCLA, I didn't interview with investment banks and consulting firms like my classmates did, because Nova Stylings made me an offer of money and responsibility I couldn't refuse.

Working for Nova was one of the best decisions I ever made, because the CEO of the company, Marty Gruber, taught me one of the most valuable skills I ever learned: how to sell. Jewelry is made of commodities—expensive commodities, but commodities nonetheless. As such, the ability to sell is crucial to success in that line of work.

The jewelry business is also hand-to-hand combat. It is different from the black magic of modern times involving search-engine optimization, A/B testing, big data, and email lists. In the jewelry business, you haven't been a salesperson until a buyer for a jewelry store sticks your product on a scale, figures out how much gold is in it, and offers to pay you 10 percent over scrap value in 120 days.

In my six years in the jewelry business, I never heard the words "partnership" or "strategic" once. On the other hand, I heard the phrase "I can get the same designs for 50 percent cheaper" every day. In other words, the jewelry business was tougher than the tech business.

Wisdom

Learn how to sell. Life is sales. Was this analog skill valuable in the tech world? Absolutely. Tasks such as evangelizing new products, raising capital, and recruiting employees are also hand-to-hand combat. I would not have succeeded without this skill set.

Earn people's trust. In the jewelry industry, retailers and their customers have to trust that the purity of the gold and the color, cut, and clarity of the diamonds are what you say they are. Three years after I left the business, I asked Tivol of Kansas City, a customer of Nova Stylings, to send me a $16,000 diamond to consider as an engagement ring. A few days later the diamond arrived in the mail without anyone's asking me for a credit card number or deposit—all it took was my reputation.

Prove yourself. How you get in doesn't matter. What matters is what you do once you're in. My entry into Nova was counting diamonds. It was a family business: Marty Gruber and his two brothers ran the place. His dad worked in the factory. His mom and uncle packed the boxes. It was a Jewish family-run business. They treated me with the utmost kindness, respect, and generosity. In return, I worked my ass off for them. And I know more Yiddish than Japanese.

Diversify your acquaintances. The Nova workers of Mexican descent were hardworking, honest, joyous, and fantastic craftsmen—not "bad hombres," as a president of the United States once called them. If you listen to some politicians and Fox News pundits, you might dislike and distrust people with different backgrounds. But if you spend time with them, you'll probably learn that people are more similar than they are different—no matter their race, creed, religion, gender, or sexual orientation.

> **In my six years in the jewelry business, I never heard the words "partnership" or "strategic" once. On the other hand, I heard the phrase "I can get the same designs for 50 percent cheaper" every day.**

Working for a small family company was fantastic preparation for the rest of my career. So if you or your kids don't get an internship at Google, Facebook, or Apple, it's not the end of the world. In fact, you or your kids may develop a stronger foundation by *not* working in La La Land companies, with their volleyball courts and free food.

Sometimes You Work for Free

Ade Harnusa Azril, an electrical engineering undergraduate student at Institut Teknologi Bandung in Indonesia, came up with the concept for the cover of one of my books, *Enchantment.* I found him by running an online design contest.

Here's how the contest worked. I used my social media accounts to announce that I was looking for a cover design. I provided the basic specifications for the cover, such as the title and subtitle, then let anyone submit ideas. To my delight, 250 people submitted 760 designs.

I selected Azril's design and paid him $1,000. The story gets interesting because of the vitriol the contest aroused. People complained that a design contest exploited designers, and they stated they would boycott the book and tell everyone they knew not to read it.

The final cover of *Enchantment.*

Their argument was that I was able to pick from the work of 250 people but paid only one. Thus, I exploited everyone who entered the contest but did not win. Furthermore, I set a precedent that conducting a contest was acceptable, which would lead to more contests taking place and the exploitation of even more designers.

The design industry association is called the American Institute of Graphic Arts (AIGA). Per their website, the danger the AIGA sees in "spec" work, as free efforts are called, is that:

Designers risk being taken advantage of. Some clients may see this as a way to get free work; it also diminishes the true economic value of the contribution designers make toward clients' objectives.

According to "general" industry practices, a client is supposed to meet with a handful of designers, explain the project, request proposals (but not designs), and then make a choice. Only one designer works on the project, and he or she is paid for that work.

I wanted to give anyone in the world a chance to design my cover—not only people who were already bona fide "designers" and within my immediate reach. And I didn't want to limit my choices to one designer's concepts. However, these two goals crossed into unacceptable territory for many designers.

With hindsight, I would still run the contest. It enabled me to get a cover that delighted me, and I helped Azril's career as well as put some money in his pocket. I doubt that the boycott, real or threatened, had an impact on the sale of the book.

Wisdom

👍 Do what it takes and pay the price of success. Writers enter writing contests. Programmers participate in hackathons. Contestants on *America's Got Talent* don't get paid. I have given dozens of free speeches, and they led to paid ones. The sheer quantity of speeches that I've delivered helped me improve, too.

This is what it takes to get a career going. Where some see exploitation, others see opportunity. You don't want to look back on your career and say, "I could have succeeded, but I didn't want to give anything away, so I failed."

Reach out and grab opportunities and wrestle them to the ground. Do it for no pay or low pay. Exploitation can be a state of mind, just like being a victim, not pegged to compensation. TEDx, for example, doesn't pay speakers, but you should jump at the chance to speak at a TEDx event for the validation and exposure.

Unveil Your Passions

In the late 1980s, I spoke at the Pentagon Mac Users Group at, logically, the Pentagon. Major Steve Broughall had started the group to help people in the military use Macs. During my speech, I joked that I would trade a Macintosh II (then the most sought-after model) for a ride in a fighter jet.

Somehow the commander of the Alaskan Air Command learned what I had said and invited me to fly in an F-15E at the Elmendorf Air Force Base in Anchorage, Alaska. So I went to Anchorage, because riding in a fighter jet is a rare experience for anyone—military or civilian.

The best amusement park ride in the world is nothing compared to flying in a fighter jet. It was a long, involved, and mind-altering experience:

> **When the plane made a sharp turn, it felt like I was in a towel that God was wringing out.**

- There were four hours of briefing and preparation to get to the point of taking off.

- I received at least five warnings about the danger of pulling the ejection lever.
- I could barely move in the cockpit. I was scared shitless the whole time and about to throw up, too.
- When the plane made a sharp turn, it felt like I was in a towel that God was wringing out.

I don't know how fighter pilots fly, attack, and avoid at the same time. It was difficult to just sit there. The pilot let me take the stick once, and it was the most power that's ever been between my legs.

Then, to top it off, an Alaskan volcano erupted (I think it was the Mount Redoubt eruption of 1989) the day after the flight, and all airlines were grounded, so I was stuck in Alaska for a few days. The ground was covered with ash. The semi-apocalyptic ending to this experience was just perfect.

But wait, there's more. I wrote a *Macworld* magazine column about this amazing adventure in which I mentioned the joke about trading a Macintosh II for a ride. Someone who read the article took it seriously and reported my bribe to the Inspector General of the US Air Force.

> There's a file about my investigation somewhere in the air force archives.

One day I got a call from an investigator from the inspector general's office and had to do some fast talking to keep the commander and me out of trouble. There's a file about my investigation somewhere in the air force archives—someday I may try to get it via the Freedom of Information Act.

Simple Questions Yield Big Answers

In December 2015, I came across an example of an accidental innovation. There's a restaurant in Waipahu, Hawaii, called Honolulu Kitchen. Its specialty is fried *manapua*—you may know *manapua* by the more commonly used terms "pork buns" or *char siu bao*. Trust me when I tell you that it's worth driving to Waipahu to try this restaurant.

The chef's wife told me the idea for fried *manapua* happened by accident when her husband dropped one into a pot of hot oil. Rather than throwing away the *manapua*, he let it cook to see how it would taste. And the rest is Hawaiian culinary history.

Many people believe that entrepreneurs plan the evolution of their company on a linear and direct path. For example, they think that Bill Gates planned that Microsoft would sell operating systems, application software, game consoles, and enterprise software and that Steve Jobs and Steve Wozniak planned to sell computers, tablets, phones, digital music, and apps.

The truth is probably that Bill Gates wanted to get IBM's business for the IBM PC, and he wasn't looking beyond that. And Steve and Woz wanted to sell some Apple Is to the Homebrew Computer Club. The long-term plan was "until we run out of money and have to get a real job."

Wisdom

Be curious. Mistakes and failures can yield opportunities. If you have the right mind-set, the opposite of success is not failure, it's learning.

My experience is that great companies begin with these kinds of simple questions:

- "Therefore, what?" This path presents itself when you have an inkling that something is happening. For example, people will own phones with cameras on data networks. Therefore, what will happen is an explosion of photography. Result: Instagram.
- "Is there a better way?" For example, "Is there a better way to sell used goods than in garage sales?" "Is there a better way to gain access to computers than by working for a school, government agency, or large company?" Results: eBay and Apple.
- "Isn't this interesting?" Suppose you develop a drug called sildenafil to treat high blood pressure and angina. It was interesting that trial patients in Swansea, Wales, experienced penile erections. Result: Viagra.

> Fried *manapua* is not as lucrative as Apple or as sexy as Viagra,
> but if serendipity presents an opportunity, don't be proud. Take
> it. It doesn't matter how you innovate, only that you do.

Stories Trump Adjectives

Pierre Omidyar, the founder of eBay, tells this story about the origin of the company: His girlfriend at the time (now wife) collected Pez dispensers, and she needed a way to sell them online. Since there wasn't one, he started eBay.

However, Omidyar told me that this was a total bullshit story. His intention was to create a "perfect market" for the efficient pricing of goods—where the demand and supply curves intersect. This explanation, however, did not intrigue the press, so a PR person invented the Pez story.

People and companies love to use adjectives to describe what they do. I wish I had a dollar for every time I heard a pitch for a "revolutionary, patent-pending, curve-jumping, innovative, scalable, enterprise-class product created by rock-star programmers."

> I wish I had a dollar for every time I heard a pitch for a "revolutionary, patent-pending, curve-jumping, innovative, scalable, enterprise-class product created by rock-star programmers."

Because everyone goes on adjective binges, these pitches are ineffective. Adjectives would work if everyone else described his product as "slow, buggy, hard-to-use pieces of crap," but that's not what happens. Everyone claims to have a great product. Hence, the effectiveness of stories in an adjective-infested world.

For example, during the introduction of Privy, the app that enables people to create private albums of pictures and videos for small groups of people, I showed potential users and journalists how my family used the product to share the memories that were meaningful to us.

I showed them a picture of when our pug pooped inside my bathroom to illustrate the concept. This isn't exactly an Instagram, LinkedIn, or Facebook moment, but it is meaningful and funny for members of our family nonetheless.

Wisdom

Use stories, not adjectives. It's a noisy world, so there's a constant struggle to get heard and remembered. Stories are better than adjectives because they are more comprehensible, memorable, and emotive.

My recommendation is that you start your presentation with a story and then follow with a simple description of what you do.

	Story	Follow-on
eBay	My girlfriend wanted to sell her Pez dispensers.	Enable buyers and sellers to set a perfect, market-clearing price.
Apple	We wanted a personal computer we could afford.	Create a market for computers for everyone.

Canva	It was too hard for our students to learn Adobe Photoshop and Illustrator.	Enable anyone to create great graphics.

Throughout your presentation, use a customer story that illustrates how people use your product. It makes your presentation more real than hypothetical-use cases. What could be more real than dog poop on your bathroom floor?

The Action Is on the Next Curve

In July 2016, I had lunch with Tom O'Toole, at the time the chief marketing officer of United Airlines, at a restaurant called Squeeze In. He came from San Francisco to Redwood City in a cab to meet me—a journey of approximately forty miles.

Unfortunately, O'Toole didn't have enough cash ($140) to pay the fare, and the cab's credit card machine didn't work. After repeated attempts, he told the driver that he would mail him the money, and he came into the restaurant.

A few minutes later, a waitress came by to tell us that the cabdriver had checked with his dispatcher, who had told him to tell O'Toole to "go find an ATM to get cash" and pay the driver.

At this point, I gave $140 to O'Toole to pay the tab, and we both thought that the problem was solved. But in the rush of trying to get to our meeting on time, O'Toole hadn't asked for a receipt and forgot his luggage in the cab.

It took several days to track down his bags and get them returned—there's something ironic about the United CMO losing his luggage, but

I digress. (I'm glad he wasn't traveling with a guitar or dog, based on United's recent history of breaking guitars and killing dogs.)

Contrast this to the typical Lyft experience. O'Toole would have gotten out of the car, his credit card would have automatically paid the fare, and the Lyft system would have generated a receipt. O'Toole could have called or texted the driver using the Lyft app and recovered his luggage.

Wisdom

Focus on the benefits you provide, not the products and services you currently sell. Taxi companies get people from one place to another—whose car it is and who's driving it don't matter.

Kodak and Polaroid were in the business of preserving memories—not applying chemicals to film or paper. But they didn't see things this way and didn't jump on digital photography. The business lesson is to focus on the reason you exist, not how you fulfill that reason.

By the way, O'Toole never paid me back. We'll see if he reads this book and sends me the money. LOL.

The Importance of the Second Follower

Simon Sinek is the author of *Start with Why*, and his TED video presentation, "How Great Leaders Inspire Action," is popular on YouTube (with 39 million views, circa 2018). In one of his other videos, he shows a person dancing in a field. After a while, a second person joins. Others follow, until it's a full-scale celebration of people dancing like fools.

Simon's point is that sometimes the difference between a nutcase and a success is that the second adopter breaks the ice and provides social proof. The first adopter is usually early employees. The second adopter is the first customer.

This is a demonstration of the "reference-account" concept. The thinking is that if you get one well-known customer, other customers will feel comfortable buying from you, too.

I experienced this in 1984. At the time, Apple was trying to break out of the K-12 education and hobbyist market served by the Apple II and sell Macs to businesses. Wishing for something doesn't make it come true, though. On many occasions, the press and potential customers asked, "What large companies are using Macintosh?"

Fortunately, there was one: Peat Marwick, now part of KPMG, the accounting and consulting behemoth. Before anyone else, it bought thousands of Macs to increase the efficiency of its field auditors. When people asked for a large-company reference account, we would pause for a few seconds as if narrowing down an extensive list and finally say, "Peat Marwick, for example."

The truth was that Peat Marwick was the *only* large company that had adopted Macintosh, besides Apple itself. This was a fake-it-till-you-make-it, Steve-Jobs-reality-distortion field at its best. The fact that Apple employees believed in Macintosh was nice, but not true validation. The second believer, Peat Marwick, was what mattered.

Also, Apple provided a level of technical support and training to Peat Marwick that would break the bank if it had to do so for every

> . . . we would pause for a few seconds as if narrowing down an extensive list and finally say, "Peat Marwick, for example."

customer. What if every customer required such special treatment to adopt your product? Part of the answer is to develop a product that doesn't need too much support, but that goal is a given.

The real-world answer is that the hard task is getting early customers to adopt your product at all. If you can succeed at this, you'll figure out a way to scale. If you don't succeed at this, it won't matter if you can scale, because you won't have customers.

Wisdom

🤙 Do whatever it takes to get your second follower. Companies, particularly start-ups, need a Peat Marwick—the second believer—to provide external validation of their product or service.

Small Changes Make a Big Difference

Authors, experts, and organizations love "strategic" decisions that take months and millions of dollars to develop. My experience is that small, simple changes can make big differences in short amounts of time at little expense. History-altering curve jumps are rare, and when they do occur, they start as small changes anyway. Here are three stories that illustrate the power of small changes:

- In 2009, the Carrillo Dining Commons on the University of California at Santa Barbara campus stopped providing trays in its all-you-can-eat facility, and food waste declined 40 percent. Trays were still available for parents getting food for kids, but people's behavior changed when it was more difficult to load up with food.

- A hospital emergency room was often overcrowded, because people would check in even though they did not need medical attention. All they wanted was a place to sleep. A doctor instituted a practice whereby people had to pay a fee of $0.25 to check in for medical treatment, and the overcrowding stopped. This nominal fee was enough to dissuade people who did not need medical care from checking in.
- Twenty-five percent of the shipping boxes of the Dutch bike company VanMoof were damaged in transit. The company developed a simple solution: printing the picture of a widescreen TV on the boxes. Damage dropped by 80 percent—apparently because workers care more about damage to TVs than to bikes.

Wisdom

Embrace small changes and "nudges" (in the words of University of Chicago economist Richard Thaler). They can make big differences despite their quick-and-dirty nature.

My experience is that "clever" almost always trumps "strategic" and expensive changes. You may wonder whether I recommend curve-jumping changes or small ones. The answer is both—and they are not mutually exclusive.

Returning to the Lyft example of a curve jump, the company also made many small changes, too. In June 2018, it integrated public transit into its app. This meant that Lyft could do more than summon a car; it could now better fill first-mile and last-mile requests.

Customer Gratification Rules

During the 2017 SXSW conference in Austin, Texas, I made a video with the chairman of Mercedes-Benz, Dieter Zetsche. The producer of the video wanted me in a plain T-shirt, so I had to scramble to find one at the last minute, since every T-shirt I own has some company's logo on it.

The closest clothing store to my hotel was a Bonobos outlet on 2nd Street, so I headed there with only thirty minutes before the recording was due to start. After walking five blocks in the heat of a sunny Austin day, I found the store and selected two T-shirts. I waited several minutes for the clerk and finally got his attention.

> **"We have to ship the shirts to you. You cannot get them here."**

First, he asked me for my email address. This was odd for a retail store, but I gave him the benefit of the doubt because I appreciate good lead generation. But then he asked me for my physical address. I asked him why, and he said, "We have to ship the shirts to you. You cannot get them here."

I was amazed. I asked him why this was the policy, and he said that if customers took delivery in the store, there wouldn't be samples to show others. I was dumbfounded. I gave him back the shirts and walked out. A block away, I found a store that did me the honor of selling and handing me a shirt.

Why Canva Succeeded

In March 2014, Peg Fitzpatrick, my coauthor on *The Art of Social Media*, was posting my tweets. She used a product called Canva to create graphics for them. The folks at Canva noticed that I used it and reached out to me via Twitter.

I wasn't sure what Peg was using for my tweets, so I had to verify with her that Canva was indeed it. I also had to ask her if I should help the company. A few weeks later, Melanie Perkins and Cliff Obrecht, two of the three cofounders of Canva, and Zach

Within a few weeks of our meeting, I signed on as Canva's chief evangelist.

Melanie Perkins and Cliff Obrecht, two of the cofounders of Canva, demonstrating their product on the day we met for the first time.

Kitschke, the company's marketing guy, were in the United States, so we met at my house.

I liked them and what they were trying to do: democratize design. They had a good story: Perkins was an instructor at the University of Western Australia and noticed that Adobe Illustrator and Photoshop were too hard to learn and too expensive to buy. Within a few weeks of our meeting, I signed on as Canva's chief evangelist.

Fast-forward to January 2018, and Canva closed a round of financing that valued the company at $1 billion. (A billion-dollar valuation is the threshold for becoming a "unicorn.") Though it's lofty territory, such a valuation is no guarantee of success, and the value of stock options is not the same as real money.

But it's a lot better to own stock options in a unicorn than to not. This is what had to happen for me to become the chief evangelist of Canva:

- Fitzpatrick had to find, use, and like Canva. Then she had to use it for my Twitter account, not only her own.
- Perkins, Obrecht, or Kitschke had to follow me on Twitter and notice that I was using their product.
- One of them had to tweet at me.
- I had to notice the tweet. This isn't as simple as it sounds, because hundreds of people were mentioning me in their tweets back then.
- I had to respond to their tweet in a manner that started a conversation.
- They had to be in the United States shortly thereafter—because I'm not known for my attention span and recollection of social media encounters.

If you multiply the probability of each step to derive the overall likelihood of my joining Canva, the number is close to zero. In other words, I became the chief evangelist because of a humongous amount of good fortune and serendipity!

But it gets even more improbable: Canva then had to progress from an unknown start-up in Sydney, Australia, to unicorn status. The probability of a start-up becoming a unicorn is also close to zero, but Canva's achievement was not because of luck. And there are important lessons there:

- Perkins and Obrecht foresaw two changes: first, text alone doesn't work well on most forms of communication, so more people needed to create graphics; second, these people could not afford the cost of nor allocate the time to learn expensive and complex high-end products.

- Canva did not merely take market share from existing high-end products, it created new types of customers who would not, or thought they could not, design graphics before. In short, Canva made the pie bigger for design, just like Apple made the pie bigger for personal computers.

- Canva has relentlessly pursued perfection. I have never worked for an organization that is more obsessed with optimizing everything—from the onboarding process to the selection of templates to technical support to localization in dozens of languages to smartphone versions to the printing of designs. I mean *never*—and I've worked for some very good companies.

Wisdom

Listen to the people who you work with. They probably know more than you do. Without Fitzpatrick, I would not have become the chief evangelist of Canva. Lots of things had to align for me to work for a company like Canva, but it all started with her.

Take chances. There was no guarantee that Canva would become such a success. After the fact, people like to say they "knew" something would succeed, but this is selective memory and reality distortion. How many times did they know something that didn't come true?

> Get ready for a marathon. Starting a company is not a sprint. It's not as simple as creating a product, selling it, and cashing out. Entrepreneurship is a marathon combined with a decathlon—that is, you have to do a lot of things well for a long time.

Ignoring Is Bliss

A large European conglomerate sent a contingent of its top executives to Silicon Valley in 2017. The goal was to learn about entrepreneurship, innovation, and the "Silicon Valley way"—as if we have magical pixie dust here, but that's another story.

I was the first person with whom they met, and my role was to provide an introduction to the region. I used these eleven points to explain the Silicon Valley phenomenon:

1. We don't know any more than you do.
2. We believe that anything is possible.
3. We fake it until we make it.
4. We forgive and forget failure.
5. We hate bureaucracy.
6. We succeed when we build what we want to use.
7. We are engineering-centric.
8. We change our minds all the time.
9. We confuse correlation and causation.
10. We declare victory retroactively.
11. We believe we can change the world.

After my presentation, we went outside and posed for a group picture behind a Mercedes-Benz. I posted this picture to Facebook and LinkedIn—generating much engagement. So far, so good—a win-win for me, because I was a Mercedes-Benz brand ambassador, and a win for the company, because a picture depicting your employees learning about innovation in Silicon Valley is good branding.

However, one random person on LinkedIn expressed surprise that the company allowed me to post a picture containing a brand that the company did not sell. Based on one observation, despite dozens of likes and positive comments by others, the company asked me to remove the picture.

Wisdom

Sweat the big stuff and ignore the chatter—especially on social media. After all I told them about believing anything is possible, getting to the next curve of innovation, forgiving failure, and hating bureaucracy, the company was leery of a picture of its employees behind a product it didn't sell.

I found this ironic. The company went through so much expense and trouble to expose its managers to Silicon Valley but couldn't cope with a single comment. And that comment wasn't even negative. Compared to the challenges that companies face, this one was inconsequential.

How I Got Every Job of My Career

The stories of how I got several of my jobs are sprinkled throughout this book, but in order to enhance pattern recognition, here's a complete list in one place.

- Truck driver's helper. Hicks Homes. Honolulu, Hawaii. Summers of 1971 and 1972. Nepotism: my uncle was the accountant for the firm.
- Filing clerk. Stanford Music Library. Stanford, California. 1973. Applied to a job listing.
- Researcher. Hawaii Commission on Crime. Honolulu, Hawaii. 1976–1977. Nepotism: my father was a friend of the lieutenant governor of Hawaii.
- Diamond counter. Nova Stylings. Los Angeles, California. 1977–1979. Nepotism: friend of a friend hired me.
- Vice president of sales and marketing. Nova Stylings. Los Angeles, California. 1979–1983. Transition from part time to full time.
- Director of marketing. Edu-Ware Services. Agoura Hills, California. 1983. Pitched the company at a trade show.
- Software evangelist. Apple. Cupertino, California. 1983–1987. Nepotism: hired by Mike Boich, my Stanford classmate, who was Apple's first software evangelist.
- CEO. ACIUS. Cupertino, California. 1987–1989. Cofounder with people I worked with at Apple.

- CEO. Fog City Software. Menlo Park, California. 1993–1995. Cofounder with friends.
- Chief evangelist. Apple. Cupertino, California. 1995–1997. Quasi-nepotism: someone I knew at Apple reached out to me.
- CEO. Garage.com. Palo Alto, California. 1998–2008. Approached by an industry figure to cofound the company.
- Special advisor to the CEO. Motorola (when it was a division of Google). Sunnyvale, California. 2013–2014. Nepotism: a friend who worked at Apple who became an executive at Google reached out to me.
- Chief evangelist. Canva. Sydney, Australia. 2014–present. Canva reached out to me after seeing I used its product.
- Brand ambassador. Mercedes-Benz. Stuttgart, Germany. 2015–present. I reached out to Mercedes-Benz to get a factory tour, and one thing led to another. (More details below.)
- Board member. Cheeze. Dubai, UAE. 2018–present. The founder of Cheeze was in the Apple store in Palo Alto looking for headphones. He got to talking to Baha Cinar, the store manager, about his product, and Cinar suggested that he talk to me. Cinar called me, and I agreed to meet.

The Mercedes-Benz brand ambassador position merits more details. I went to Berlin to make a speech for Russell Reynolds, the headhunting firm. While I was in Germany, I wanted to visit the Mercedes-Benz factory, so I reached out to some Mercedes-Benz folks who I had met at SXSW a month earlier.

I got a VIP tour of the production line of the AMG GT. After I got back, I covered the earth with social media posts about my visit and I offered to help Mercedes-Benz with my tech and press contacts, as well as make speeches without any quid pro quo arrangement.

Wisdom

First, foster connections, not job applications. The only job that I got through an ad was the filing clerk position at the Stanford Music Library. The rest of the jobs came about because of my personal relationships or because people knew of me. Note: knew *of* me, not knew me. It's not who you know; it's who knows you.

Pay it forward. My uncompensated help and offers of assistance led to a closer relationship with Mercedes-Benz and eventually the brand-ambassador position. I did this before there was any talk of compensation.

Over the years I've had many conversations with people along these lines: "If the company would pay me, give me surfboards, give me Macs, or provide me with a free Sprinter van, I could really help it." The logic was always, "I don't want to get screwed. The company has to do something first: I know I will be great."

Life doesn't work this way. Companies get pitched every day with people who say they can do great things if they get paid or freebies. Few people start helping and worry about developing a financial relationship later. The upside of paying it forward usually far outweighs the downside of being exploited.

06

Values

*It's not hard to make decisions when you
know what your values are.*

—Roy Disney

Over the course of my lifetime, apart from episodic deviations for cars,
I had two primary goals: first, to raise four kids who are joyful, productive, and socially responsible; second, to empower people to change the
world. Here are the experiences that led me to these goals.

Honor Counts

Back in the late 1980s, America Online began life as AppleLink Personal Edition, an Apple-labeled online service for consumers that

Apple contracted Quantum Computer Services to create. However, Apple blew up this contract for unknown reasons—if nothing else, this proved that Apple wasn't omniscient, as AOL went on to become a massive success.

On the day that Apple ended the Quantum relationship in 1989, I had dinner with Steve Case, the founder of Quantum, and his team. They were in a state of shock and down in the dumps. But I told them that Apple's decision could be the best thing that ever happened to them, because they were now free to create an independent company and get off Apple's teats.

Out of desperation more than anything else, Case asked me if I would do some consulting and online conferences for $2,000 per month, plus stock options. I agreed, and for the next few months I helped out, until my contact at AOL stopped asking.

I saw Case several years later, and he asked me if AOL was still paying me and had given me the stock options. I told him I hadn't done much work, so the company wasn't paying me, and I had never gotten the stock. I told him to "forget about it."

Nonetheless, he insisted that I get the stock, so I received options for two thousand shares. The stock split several times and the per-share price rose like a rocket, so these options became my version of the proverbial two fish and five loaves of bread in the Bible.

To put this into perspective, I made approximately $250,000 from Apple stock over my career. So I could make the case that the company I did the most work for provided the least money, and the company that I did the least work for provided the most.

The only reason I made any money from AOL stock is that Case was an honorable person; he did not have to grant me those options. There was no legal paperwork that proved he ever offered them to me in the first place.

Here's another story of above-and-beyond honor. This time the honorable guys were Patrick Lor and Bruce Livingston, the cofounders of iStockphoto, a Calgary company that sold stock photos at one-twentieth the price of companies like Getty.

I met Lor at the September 2003 Banff Venture Forum, where I was a speaker. The topic that brought us together was not entrepreneurship, venture capital, or photography. It was ice hockey.

As I am prone to do, I diverged from the topic of my speech to discuss my passion for hockey—what better way to bond with a Canadian audience? I mentioned that I had visited the Graf factory in Calgary the day before and ordered a pair of skates. Nike had given me a pair just before I left my home for Calgary, so I now had an extra pair.

In the middle of my speech about entrepreneurship, I mentioned this extra pair and asked if anyone wanted to buy them. Years later, Patrick told me that he really didn't need the skates nor did he have the money to purchase them, but he bought them as a way to meet and talk with me at the conference.

We spoke about more than just the skates that day, and he asked me to join his company's board of advisors. I agreed, but we never came to a formal agreement because of the complexities of Canadian law. Regardless, I evangelized the company for several years.

Getty eventually bought iStockphoto for $50 million (US). Patrick and Bruce made more money than they ever dreamed possible, and they contacted me with the question, "How much stock should we have granted you if we had a formal deal?"

My answer was that a typical advisor would get .5 percent for a role such as advisor, spokesperson, or window dressing. I did all three. And what did Patrick and Bruce do? They paid me 1.5 percent of the purchase price from their share of the deal! That was another chunk of money I never saw coming.

As this and the Steve Case story show, I made out just fine without formal contracts. A logical question is, "Why did these two situations turn out so well?" Several reasons:

- I'm a lucky guy.
- I was usually in a position of power and visibility, so it would have been dumb to shortchange me.
- They were honorable people.

Of these reasons, the last one is the best explanation.

Wisdom

Do the right thing. Be a Steve, Patrick, or Bruce. A formal contract with a dishonorable person is worth less than an informal contract with an honorable one. These guys taught me about honor when honor meant giving up hundreds of thousands of dollars.

There's Dishonor, Too

I wish I could tell you I've never been screwed in a business deal—that life is all unicorns, pixie dust, Steve Cases, Patrick Lors, and Bruce Livingstons. It's not true. There are crooks in the world, too, and I have been screwed three times in my career. Speaking agents were the perpetrators in two cases.

This is how the speaking business works: The event host, usually a large company or organization, uses a speaking agency to select speakers and manage their appearances. The payment flow is from the client to the agency.

The client pays the entire fee before the event occurs, because there is little leverage to get them to pay once an event is over. The agency keeps its 20 to 25 percent and pays the balance to the speaker only after the event. The thinking is that the agency is protecting the client in case the speaker doesn't show up or performs poorly. This system works as long as the speaking agency is solvent and honorable.

There's the catch. Both agencies screwed me by using payments from my speeches to pay other speakers and payments for other speakers to pay me. For this scheme to work, large sums of money must constantly flow through the agency. Like the game of musical chairs, if the music stops, someone can get caught without a seat.

In the two cases where I was not paid, I should have seen the scams coming. Both started with payments that were days, then weeks, then months late. Both agencies lied to me; the litany of excuses included the client's not paying, the bank's making a mistake, a medical emergency, a family emergency, a divorce—ad nauseam. I trusted them for far too long.

At the end of my working relationship with one of the agencies, a test of *my* honor occurred. In this case, a client had fully paid for a speech. The agency never paid me. There were two choices: take the speech, knowing that I'd never get paid, or refuse to make the speech, knowing that I'd never get paid.

I made the speech. It wasn't the client's fault that I wouldn't get paid. And no matter how defensible my choosing not to appear may have been, my reputation would have taken a hit—"Guy Kawasaki might not show up for a speech"—and that was unacceptable.

As for the third rip-off, it happened after I left Apple the second time to cofound a company called Garage.com, a venture capital investment bank—meaning it helped entrepreneurs raise money from investors. Our business model was to receive 7 percent of the money we helped raise plus stock in the companies that obtained funding.

We helped one new business raise money from a venture capital firm. At the close of the deal, a partner in the firm threatened to back out of the deal if the company intended to pay the fees it owed Garage.com. He did not want any of his firm's money to be spent banking our fees.

The CEO of the company was caught in the middle: honor our deal or lose the financing. Guess what happened. I understand why the CEO took the money and did not pay us. In fact, we let him violate his contract because we didn't want the company to die. But what the partner at the venture capital firm did was a bullshit power play. He knew he could squeeze us because he was the big dog at the table.

Wisdom

Try to avoid arrangements where people receive your money as your agent, take their share, and then send you the rest. As the saying goes, possession is nine-tenths of the law. Lawsuits and even criminal actions seldom rectify a bad situation.

However, some arrangements involving other parties receiving your money are unavoidable. Even after my bad experiences, I chose to use a literary agency and a speaking agency. In both cases I went with large, established organizations that were far more stable than "an agent with a secretary and a few salespeople."

Verify any excuses at the second sign (let the first one slide) of trouble. For example, in the case of "client didn't pay," call the client; if the "bank made a mistake," call the bank; if the "wire transfer takes a week," call the bank, etc. Verify every excuse.

If you catch the company lying, take immediate and severe action. If you don't have the stomach for this (I don't), then find a surrogate to be the bad guy. In my case, I should have refused to book any new speeches until past debts were paid, and I should have immediately ended my exclusive relationship with the agencies.

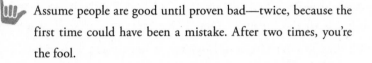 Assume people are good until proven bad—twice, because the first time could have been a mistake. After two times, you're the fool.

Deliver bad news early if you are on the other side of such a situation and are experiencing difficulty. Then try to work out a way to make good on your commitments. At least this shows you're an honest person who is trying and not an out-and-out crook.

Do the right thing, not what you can get away with when you achieve a position of power and wealth. Money can't buy scruples—indeed, money may *prevent* scruples. With money comes the responsibility to act magnanimous—not abusive. Remember this if you get rich.

Nerds Rule

In 1985, I gave a summer job to an undergraduate from USC (the first and last time I helped anyone from USC, because of my Stanford and UCLA pedigree). His task was to write sample assembly language programs for Macintosh. We provided his programs to

Macintosh developers so they could see how to use this software development path.

Don't worry if you don't know what assembly language is, because it isn't important to the story. This kid was tall, heavy, and fair-skinned. He was slightly pushy and obnoxious, as most of us are when we are young, and he was from Hillsborough, one of Northern California's wealthiest areas.

We nicknamed him the Hillsborough Doughboy. In case you're not familiar with the Pillsbury Doughboy, he's the character that jumps out of the Pillsbury Crescent Rolls can in television commercials. He is soft, white, and jovial.

The Hillsborough Doughboy grew up to be not only a man, but *the* Man.

Fast-forward a few decades, and the Hillsborough Doughboy started Salesforce.com. Yes, the Hillsborough Doughboy is Marc Benioff. He made billions of dollars, but more telling, he became a generous philanthropist. For example, he donated $200 million to the UCSF hospital system.

The Hillsborough Doughboy grew up to be not only a man, but *the* Man. I like to think I helped his career in a tiny way by giving him that summer job.

And the Man is not just rich and successful—he also has class. In 2015, I emailed him to ask him to help Mike Boich's son get a job at Salesforce.com. Boich was running evangelism in the Macintosh Division and was my boss when Benioff was an intern, so Boich was Benioff's boss's boss. Thirty years later Marc reciprocated by helping Boich's son.

Then, in 2016, I asked Benioff to help my son Nic get a job at Salesforce.com, too, and within three hours of the request, he told his head of global recruiting to get involved. Within a few weeks Nic was

Hanging with Marc Benioff.

a Salesforce employee, so Benioff reciprocated twice to his Apple colleagues from decades earlier.

Most people at Benioff's level would not answer the email, not remember what I had done, or not feel the need to reciprocate. As I said, Benioff has class. And two generations of Kawasakis got their start thanks to nepotism.

Wisdom

Help people and be generous. It's good karma, and the nerdy punk intern may someday inherit, if not rule, the earth. Plus, your kids may need jobs.

Take the high road: if people help you, reciprocate. They may mention you in their book someday. And you'll find out there's not much traffic on the high road.

Humility Rocks

In 2008, Richard Branson and I spoke at a conference in Moscow, Russia. This was the first time we met. We were in the speaker prep room, and he asked me if I flew on Virgin—which is what you would expect him to ask.

I explained that I was a Global Services–level United Airlines customer—which meant free automatic upgrades and other VIP services (but not repayment of taxi fares). No one except United employees knows what it takes to achieve this exclusive status. Reaching it is not as simple as accumulating lots of miles.

Then Richard Branson dropped to his knees and started polishing my shoes with his coat.

I explained to Branson that I didn't want to jeopardize my Global Services status by flying on other airlines. Then Richard Branson dropped to his knees and started polishing my shoes with his coat. That was the moment I decided to start flying on Virgin America. (I never saw Steve Jobs get on his knees to get a customer.)

Richard Branson polishing my shoes so that I would fly on Virgin.

How I Tried to Help Hillary

I've been wrong about many things, but nothing comes close to my belief that Hillary Clinton would trounce Donald Trump in the 2016 presidential election. Hundreds of experts have tried to explain her loss, and I can't offer an explanation of what she did wrong, but I do have several stories about her campaign.

First, my family attended her fund-raiser in Los Altos, California, on November 4, 2015. This was the first time I had seen her in person, and I was impressed with her intelligence and sense of humor.

I broadcast her speech live on Facebook until I was told to stop because video recording wasn't permitted. Say what? Tens of thousands of people watched my Facebook Live events back then, so this was a lost opportunity.

After she spoke, we lined up with five hundred other fans to take a picture with her. People were hustled in to spend approximately fifteen seconds with her, and a staff photographer took the photo. No one was

Hanging with Hillary Clinton.

permitted to take selfies or hand his camera to someone on her staff to take photos.

I knew one of her volunteers, so I was able to obtain a copy of the photo taken by the staff photographer to use on my social media. I don't know if most people got a copy, because no one was recording who was in the photos.

At the time, I figured that this procedure was in the interest of speed. I've been photographed enough to know that people fumble around with their phone for a long time before they take a picture. But each group could have handed one phone to a staffer to take a photo at the same time as the staff photographer.

Some quick math: Instead of permitting only a staff photo that people never received, members of the audience that night could have handed their phone to one of the many millennial staffers who were standing around. Almost everyone at this event was using an iPhone, so little training would have been necessary.

Let's say that 500 people had, on average, 1,000 followers each. This means that 500,000 people could have seen a friend's or family member's photo with Hillary Clinton on Twitter, Facebook, Instagram, or Google+. I assume this procedure was repeated at other appearances, so the lost exposure was easily in the tens of millions.

After the event I made three offers to talk to the Clinton campaign staff about the use of social media. Each time the response was that the campaign didn't want my help.

Fast-forward to 2018. On separate occasions I met with executives at Microsoft and Facebook. We talked about how their companies interacted with the presidential campaigns. Both executives told me that they and their company colleagues were Clinton supporters and had wanted to help above and beyond their job responsibilities.

And both told me the Clinton campaign turned down their offers to help. By contrast, the Trump campaign accepted all the help that was offered by these companies. And you know how the presidential election of 2016 turned out.

Wisdom

Eat when served. I'm not saying that if the Clinton campaign had let me broadcast live and take a selfie, Hillary would have won. But the policy was indicative of an attitude akin to hubris. And if her campaign had accepted help from the likes of Microsoft and Facebook, the results might well have been different.

Was it arrogance, shortsightedness, or understandable prioritization that made her campaign turn down the offers of assistance? We'll never know, but I learned several things from this debacle:

- Nothing is over until it's over.
- Polls don't mean anything.
- If someone with more than 10 million followers offers to help you, you should probably accept the help.
- If Microsoft and Facebook offer to help, you should accept their help.
- If there's anything worse than not getting help when you need it, it's not accepting help when it's offered.

The World Is a Big Place

This story was in my baccalaureate speech to Palo Alto High School, but it merits repeating and further explanation. I made a mistake in college: I graduated early. I entered Stanford with AP credits, and I took a heavy course load. This enabled me to fulfill my requirements by December 1975, even though the school year ended in June 1976.

I attribute my early graduation to my DAA (Diligent Asian Approach), which involves studying hard and forgoing extracurricular activities that don't look good on a college application. It's the philosophy of "start violin at two, enter the Kumon math program at five, take calculus in the seventh grade, and start a nonprofit at fifteen to get into Stanford or Harvard."

I should have taken the full four years—or even more—to graduate. I regret not attending any of the Stanford overseas campuses or at least traveling outside the United States. Today, at sixty-three, with one wife, four kids, one dog, eight chickens, one job, one brand ambassadorship, one fellowship, and one directorship, I have little desire to travel for pleasure.

I made a mistake in college: I graduated early.

The theory of seeing the world as a tourist when you're an empty-nester doesn't apply, because my youngest child is thirteen. He'll be in college in seven years, so I'll be pushing seventy, if not pushing flowers out of the ground, when he moves out. And by then there may be grandchildren from my other kids, so I won't want to travel.

Wisdom

See the world when you're young. The time to do this is when you don't have a mortgage, car payments, or kids (though maybe student loans). There's not going to be a better time to travel.

I have never met anyone who wished they had started working earlier.

I could also make the case that seeing the world will make you a better employee or entrepreneur. This is why it's good to travel while you're young and not wait until you're mid-career or retired. I predict that you'll come to three conclusions:

- People around the world are more similar than they are different.
- Your life is better than most people's.
- Traffic where you live is not as bad as you thought.

Email Doesn't Matter

I once lost four hundred unanswered emails in my inbox because my email application crashed. Afterward no one sent a follow-up email asking why I hadn't responded. Later I lost another inbox, and only a handful of people followed up.

Those episodes led me to realize that I was driving myself crazy trying to answer hundreds of emails that people didn't care about. If the issue wasn't important enough for them to follow up on, why should I bother to answer?

> **. . . when friends died, I would delete everything in my inbox . . .**

When I turned fifty years old, some of my friends started dying; the first one was a buddy named Jos Henkens. This is macabre, but I adopted the practice that when friends died, I would delete everything in my inbox that was more than thirty days old, and then I would spend more time with my family for the following weeks.

I don't know of any negative results because of this practice, and I've done it several more times when people in my life have passed away.

Wisdom

Establish your priorities. I'm not suggesting that you adopt this morbid practice, but answering email is less important than you think. You only live once, and only briefly, so choose how you spend your time. Anyone who really wants to get in touch with you will follow up multiple times.

Canadians Are the Best People

In May 2010, I gave a speech at the National Grocery Conference in Halifax, Nova Scotia. During the speech, the left side of my chest started to ache. When I was done, I told my hosts about the pain, and an emergency medical technician named Ed Lundrigan insisted that I see a doctor.

So off I went to the Queen Elizabeth II hospital, accompanied by Aran Hamilton, a friend who was hosting me that day. Within an hour of arriving, I saw three doctors and was diagnosed with pneumonia, not a heart attack.

By then I had missed my Air Canada flight to Toronto (the last one of the day), as well as my connecting flight to San Francisco. But here's where the story gets good. My hosts put the word out to see if there was a way to get me to Toronto that night so I could catch the morning flight to San Francisco.

Then they arranged for me to fly on the private jet of Mike McCain, the CEO of Maple Leaf Foods, who was in Halifax for the same conference. Aran and I grabbed our bags and off we went to the private-jet terminal.

Mike met us at the airport, and we flew to Toronto. The next morning, I caught a plane to San Francisco and lived happily ever after. Whether you're trapped in an embassy in Tehran or getting medical treatment in Halifax, nobody takes care of you like Canadians.

> Whether you're trapped in an embassy in Tehran or getting medical treatment in Halifax, nobody takes care of you like Canadians.

More Canadian goodness: I received the bill from the hospital three weeks later, and it was for a grand total of $900 CAD—roughly $700 USD at the time. That amount would get you an aspirin and a patient gown in a US hospital; the total bill in the United States would have been at least $20,000.

Wisdom

Memorize this: "Canadians. Are. The. Best!"

What Are You Going to Tell Your Grandchildren?

In October 2016, I went to Berlin to speak to the marketing staff of Mercedes-Benz. The night before my speech, I had dinner with two German friends, and the conversation inevitably turned to the presidential election in the United States. At this point, thirty days before the election, few people believed Donald Trump would win.

The very fact that Trump was one of the two leading candidates astounded us. My friends told me that they still didn't understand how their grandparents' generation could let Adolf Hitler come to power, and they saw direct parallels between Hitler and Trump.

They warned me, "If Trump wins, it will be 1933 for America." What they meant was that before Hitler was Hitler, he was "just" a popular politician. He didn't start killing Jewish people and invading countries on his first day as chancellor.

This conversation had a profound effect on me. I didn't want my grandchildren to wonder if I resisted Trump, so I started using my social media accounts to #resist him. Few, if any, social media influencers took such an aggressive stance at the time. They didn't want to go off-topic from their usual subjects such as food, cats, fashion, social media, or entrepreneurship, because taking such a stance might affect their brand and cause them to lose followers. But the fear of losing followers and business were not a strong enough deterrent for me to keep silent, so I turned my Facebook, Twitter, Google+, and even LinkedIn accounts into political feeds—contrary to the wisdom of so-called social media experts. And guess what?

While a few hundred people complained about me getting political and resisting Trump, the feedback was far and away supportive. Here are two examples:

> ". . . you are Guy Fuckin' Kawasaki. Who gives a shit about losing some followers b/c of something you write? Your power comes from your vast experience, by you being right and you being early. Don't change from those three things."

> "I'm not willing to bring politics into my LinkedIn feed but I wholeheartedly agree with you. In fact, your persistent outspoken

> But the fear of losing followers and business were not a strong enough deterrent for me to keep silent, so I turned my Facebook, Twitter, Google+, and even LinkedIn accounts into political feeds— contrary to the wisdom of so-called social media experts.

commentary has me questioning my own unwillingness to step up . . ."

I may have lost a few thousand followers, but I gained tens of thousands more. Standing up for what I believe was not only the right thing to do, it also was a good marketing decision, because my brand was aligned with democracy and meritocracy, not the Trump Reich. However, even if my stance had cost me followers, branding, or income, I would have still done it. That is what I will tell my grandchildren.

Wisdom

Do what's right. Influence comes with a moral obligation to stand up for your principles and to help less fortunate people. This may come with personal and short-term costs—but that's what a moral obligation entails.

It Could Be Worse

Ménière's disease is a combination of hearing loss, tinnitus (ringing in the ear), and vertigo. I have had it since approximately 1993. There is no cure for the disease as of 2018. The medical treatment is a shotgun approach:

- Reduce intake of salt, caffeine, and alcohol.
- Reduce water retention by taking a diuretic such as Dyazide.

- Reduce stress (as if you can easily choose to experience less stress).
- Take anti-anxiety drugs such as Ativan.

The theory is that salt, caffeine, alcohol, stress, and anxiety might cause Ménière's. I have a different theory: my Ménière's is a result of listening to hundreds of crappy pitches from entrepreneurs. They all promised curve-jumping, patent-pending, first-mover, scalable unicorn companies.

I came to view Ménière's as the worst of the best diseases—because it's a pain in the ass, but it doesn't kill you. (A Ménière's sufferer once described the tinnitus component of the disease by saying that God was trying to talk to him, but She didn't send him a modem to process the signal.)

Wisdom

Be thankful. As I write this book, Ménière's is the worst ailment that has affected me. Steve Jobs and his family would gladly have traded pancreatic cancer for a little hearing loss, tinnitus, and vertigo.

Look for good news. There is no known cure for Ménière's, but I'm convinced that the steps I've taken to treat it have extended my life. I haven't added salt to food in decades. I seldom drink any alcohol. (Caffeine, however, I haven't reduced.) I take Dyazide every day, so my blood pressure is at the level of a teenager's.

Be patient. There is no known cure for Ménière's as I write this, but someday there will be. No amount of money or number of

> social media followers can buy me the solution before it's found. For a long time, this was frustrating for a Silicon Valley guy who believed that everything has a cause and therefore must have a cure to accept.

The Tests of Life

Over my career, I developed a handful of tests to help me make decisions. They provided a cogent and long-lasting structure to determine right and wrong, good and bad.

Wikipedia/NPR Donation Test. Imagine a website that thrusts an ugly banner in front of you every time you visit for several weeks. This banner is not only ugly, it asks for money.

And yet these banners work well. To wit, Wikipedia raised more than $77 million from donations in 2016. These banners work because people love Wikipedia for the value it provides, so people not only tolerate the banner but open up their wallets.

NPR does something similar: interrupting its content with fundraising telethons several times a year. NPR provides such great content that people not only tolerate the interruption but open their wallets. In 2016, NPR received approximately $90 million in contributions, grants, and corporate sponsorships.

Provide value. The Wikipedia/NPR Donation Test determines whether you provide something of such value that people will gladly reciprocate in some manner. This test isn't only about soliciting donations—it's a framework for life in general. How much good do you do for people?

If you provide value, you can ask for—and receive—reciprocation. This is the glue that holds society together. You may not care about reciprocation, but the important concept is to help people so much that they would gladly reciprocate.

Re-share Test. I came up with this test to help people judge whether something is worth posting on social media, but it has broader implications about the standards that you hold yourself up to. In the social media context, people share what they think their followers, friends, and fans will appreciate: pictures, videos, essays, and links. Such content passes the *share* test—that is, you think your own content is good enough to share.

A tougher test is whether people like your content so much that they *re-share* it to their family, friends, colleagues, and followers. It's one thing to eat at a restaurant. It's another to tell other people to eat there. When people recommend a restaurant or re-share your post, they risk their reputation.

Shopping Center Test. Suppose you saw someone at a shopping center, but that person did not see you. You have three choices: (1) rush over to the person and say hello; (2) see if happenstance brings you face-to-face; or (3) go to another shopping center.

Your choice reveals much about the person: You'd rush over to greet the right person. You wouldn't take the initiative for a so-so person. You would run from someone you didn't like. This is a useful test to apply to your acquaintances, job applicants, and family.

So-What? Test. If you let it, drama can fill your life. My experiences have led me to conclude that trying to eliminate drama is futile—what is important is how you react when drama occurs.

For example, when I joined the board of a nonprofit organization, we experienced drama every week when some part of the organization's employees and customers didn't like a board decision.

The sequence was that we would make a decision and then several dozen employees or customers would freak out, then the board would freak out that employees or customers freaked out and rush to try to appease them (never succeeding), then another drama would occur and the cycle would start again. This happened once a month for my entire tenure.

The reason the board freaked out is that they imagined apocalyptic, worst-case, or at least bad-case, scenarios: employees would quit, employees would strike, customers would abandon us, and the *New York Times*, the *Wall Street Journal*, and the *Washington Post* would write a front-page exposé. None of these things occurred.

From this experience, I derived the So-What? Test. It means when drama occurs, you ask yourself, "So what?" For example, your daughter got a C on a math test. So what? She won't have a 4.0 GPA. So what? She won't get into Dartmouth. So what? She will not succeed in life.

Really? Getting into Dartmouth determines the outcome of her life? I don't think so. (There's a lot more about parenting in the next chapter.)

> It means when drama occurs, you ask yourself, "So what?"

Wisdom

Ask, "So what?" This may not help prevent or avoid problems, but it will help put "crises" into perspective, and perspective is everything if you want a joyful and productive life. This doesn't mean you shouldn't work hard, but if everything doesn't go as planned, ask yourself, "So what?" a few times and see if it matters.

07

Parenting

A child can teach an adult three things: to be happy for no reason, to always be busy with something, and to know how to demand with all his might that which he desires.

—Paulo Coelho

Parenting has been the most challenging and the most rewarding activity of my life. Nothing has brought me more joy than my family. At the end of my career, I want people to remember me as a father—not an entrepreneur, author, speaker, brand ambassador, evangelist, or influencer.

A Bit About My Family

My wife's name is Beth Kawasaki. We met at Apple in 1983 through another Apple employee named Sandi Vargas. You're probably skeptical about stories of love at first sight, but this was absolutely the case for me.

Beth and I have four kids: Nicodemus (1993), Noah (1995), Nohemi (2001), and Nathan (2005). They have been the greatest source of joy in our lives. Nothing else comes close. They are our four little start-ups, and circa 2018, here's a description of each of them.

Nicodemus graduated from the University of California, Berkeley, in 2016 with a degree in economics. A few days after graduation, he moved to Sydney, Australia, to play ice hockey for the Sydney Bears and to work for the University of New South Wales. He returned to the United States and went to work for Salesforce.com in 2017 (as you learned from my Marc Benioff story). In 2018, he moved to Los Angeles to pursue a career as a user-interface designer.

Noah graduated from the University of California, Los Angeles, with a major in economics. After a brief fling with rugby at UCLA, he set his sights higher by taking up skydiving and wingsuit flying. He insists that the riskiest part of skydiving and wingsuiting is driving to the airport. And he promised my wife that he won't BASE jump (jumping from a fixed structure as opposed to from a plane). In the fall of 2018, he went to work for Looker, a data analytics firm in Santa Cruz.

Nohemi is our warrior woman. She provided an entirely different experience for us after we'd put two boys through high school. She is an avid surfer with a passion for digital photography and marine biology. In high school, Nohemi started a video and photography business called Her Highness Media.

Nate is Mr. Charisma. His personality fills a surf break, and because of the "bro influence" of his older male siblings, he makes tiger moms with only one child quake in their Jimmy Choos because of his bold personality. If he doesn't become a great salesman, I will be amazed.

Adoption Is a Beautiful Thing

We have three sons and one daughter. Our two older kids, both boys, are our biological children. Our younger two kids are adopted from Guatemala. This means that my wife and I have been blessed with one of the most beautiful experiences in life: adopting children. Without question, adoption is as good for the parents as it is for the children.

My life would have been much less interesting if I only had sons. For one thing, I would not have experienced the joy of watching my daughter play hockey and surf. And whereas some girls design covers for books called *How to Pick a Perfect Book*, Nohemi designed *How to Get Your Hockey Gear On*.

Then two years after adopting Nohemi, we got a call from the same orphanage notifying us that a boy was available for adoption, and he was Nohemi's brother. In for a penny, in for a pound—what a great privilege to enable siblings to grow up together! So that's how we went, in basketball jargon, from man-to-man (two parents, two kids) to zone (two parents, four kids).

Grandpa Kawasaki with his grandchildren. Left to right: Noah, Nohemi, Grandpa, Nicodemus, and Nate.

Nohemi's cover design is on the right.

Consider adopting a child. You may think that the children are the fortunate ones, but you will be blessed, too. There are few experiences more rewarding than adopting children. End of discussion.

 Understand that you don't get the full experience of parenting until the kids outnumber the adults. I highly recommend the numerical disadvantage.

So Is Keeping Your Mouth Shut

If you've ever considered adoption, I strongly encourage it. However, prepare yourself for some strange reactions. For example, shortly before the arrival of Nate, my wife and I had dinner with a friend and his wife. During the meal we told them we were adopting a second child from Guatemala.

My friend's response, though well-meaning, was, "You do know that adopted children tend to have problems, right?" My unspoken reaction was twofold: *First, what kind of asshole are you? We have already adopted a girl, and I told you we are adopting another child, not thinking of adopting again.*

> "You do know that adopted children tend to have problems, right?"

And your comment is that he's likely to have problems? Second, are you telling us that kids who are raised by their biological parents never have problems?

Some men believe that only the fruit of their loins merits parenting. They are idiots. Besides, their typical contribution to a pregnancy is only ten seconds long—five, if they are honest. Having adopted twice, I can tell you that when a caretaker places your baby in your arms at an orphanage, the origin of their DNA doesn't matter.

Wisdom

👆 Don't always express your "honest opinion." My friend's intention might have been good, but did he believe we would cancel the adoption based on his opinion? Or return our daughter? Sometimes it's best to just shut up.

There's Always a Way to Prepare

Noah failed his driving test twice. In California, if you flunk a third time, you must start the entire license application process over. This would mean getting another permit after a cooling-off period, retaking the written test, and then taking the driving test again.

To ensure that he didn't flunk a third time, I had the brilliant idea that we drive to the local Department of Motor Vehicles and watch several examiners take applicants on the road for tests. We then drove the route for practice.

Yes, Noah got a perfect score on his third try, and I earned major dad credibility—something that's not easy to achieve with teenage boys. But wait, there's more. One of my friends did the same thing with his daughter, except that the examiner noticed them following the car. The examiner stopped and confronted the father for tailing her.

As (bad) luck would have it, the same examiner was his daughter's tester. Guess what? The examiner flunked his daughter after a short distance.

Wisdom

🤙 Prepare for every test, interview, or challenge. There's always a way—for example, try searching on Quora. However, three factors often get in the way of proper preparation:

- Arrogance: "I don't need to prepare. I'll rise to the occasion."
- Laziness: "I'm too busy to prepare."
- Stupidity: "I'm probably going to fail, so I won't prepare. Then when I fail, I'll prove myself right."

People who prepare the most are the "luckiest," and preparation trumps "natural ability" almost every time. If you prepare and have natural ability, you're unbeatable.

But note that not everyone appreciates the value and propriety of good preparation, as my friend and his daughter learned.

My Life as a Lyft Driver and an ATM

My wife and I once offered Nohemi an incentive for good grades: we would buy her a miniature horse. You know how this story goes: she got the grades, of course. That's when we learned how much these horses cost and how hard it is to care for them.

Let's just say that we thought hockey was an expensive sport, but a horse, even a small one, is a hole in the universe that you pour money into. So my wife, great negotiator that she is, convinced our daughter

> **For a while I was the grandfather of thirteen chicks. Pretty fun. Pretty cool. Life was good until we discovered that two of the chicks were roosters.**

that chickens would be more fun (and cheaper).

So far, so good.

My wife and daughter found a website that sells chicks, and according to my daughter, the smallest order you could place was for a dozen. And, lucky us, when you ordered a dozen, you got a bonus chick for free.

So far, pretty good.

The chicks arrived in a box at the post office. Animal rights folks: don't come after me. I had no idea about the delivery method until after the order was placed.

For a while I was the grandfather of thirteen chicks. Pretty fun. Pretty cool. Life was good until we discovered that two of the chicks were roosters. I guess "Chicks.com" doesn't know which chicks are male and which are female.

For several months, everything was fine, but then the roosters started crowing. This was new ground for me. The concert started at three a.m. and continued all day long. I then learned that roosters are illegal in the town we live in. I started checking "Hawks.com" for a natural, organic solution.

In desperation, Beth posted a message on Facebook to see if any of her friends wanted two roosters. Two hours later, to our amazement, one friend volunteered to take both. We had to take care of this within a few days, because I expected the police to arrest me any day for disturbing the peace.

Three noisy, will-the-cops-be-knocking-on-our-door? mornings went by, and finally, it was time to drop off the birds. Alas, my wife "had to" go to a conference. Ergo, I had to drive my daughter and her two roosters to Esparto, California, in my car. Never heard of Esparto? Don't feel bad, neither had I. It's not the inspiration for any Justin Bieber songs, in case you're wondering.

It was two hours there and two hours back, on the day the California drought decided to end. My car smelled like a wet barn, and I couldn't get the stink out for weeks. It was also an experiment in whether bird diseases can cross over to humans. But the roosters could crow all they wanted in their new home, so the universe went back into balance.

Fast-forward to a few months later. The eight remaining hens, who had started out as "free range" chicks in our yard, could now fly over fences, and they decided to poop on our neighbor's tennis court as it was being staged for a party. My neighbor persuaded us that we had to get a chicken coop, and she even introduced us to a contractor.

Of course, we built them the Ritz-Carlton of chicken coops: gluten-free, organic feed and scratch in the honor bar, free Wi-Fi, yoga classes, high-definition TV—you name it. The coop cost $2,500. However, this was still way cheaper than a horse.

Wisdom

Accept that "parental control" is an illusion, if not an oxymoron. Parenting is being a Lyft driver and an ATM rolled into one. Accept this role and enjoy it while your kids are still living with you. I loved, and still love, (almost) every minute of raising my kids.

You Can Only Do So Much

Nicodemus had his special moments, too. For example, he applied to Woodside Priory, an elite college-prep school located in Woodside, California. The competition for admission was fierce—there was an overabundance of highly qualified applicants.

During his interview, he told the director of admissions that he wanted to play tackle football. At the time, Woodside didn't field a tackle football team, and he was not accepted by the school—I assume because the director of admissions knew he wanted to play football.

After this happened came one of the few times that I told any of my kids to lie—that is, if the director of admissions of a school that has ten applicants for every position asks if you have any concerns or questions, just say no, you don't have any good questions.

> **"Do you know where the ice hockey team practices?"**

Four years later, Nicodemus did something similar. This time he was applying to UCLA, and we met with one of the vice chancellors. At the end of our meeting, she asked him, "Do you have any questions about UCLA?" His response was, "Do you know where the ice hockey team practices?"

After the meeting, I pounded him: "The vice chancellor of UCLA asks you if you have any questions, and your only question is where the hockey team practices?" Come to think of it, UCLA didn't accept him, either.

On the other hand, he didn't tell my wife and me that he had applied to the University of California at Berkeley, and he got in. I'm glad we didn't visit for an interview.

You're Not the Center of the Solar System

The importance of a LinkedIn profile to job searches—and professional success in general—is now obvious. But a few years earlier, I looked at Nicodemus's profile and had seen that his avatar was cropped from a photo taken at his fraternity's winter formal.

In other words, the avatar was crap and inappropriate for LinkedIn.

I told him to change the picture, and his response was, "But I never use LinkedIn." He missed the point entirely. It didn't matter what social media platform he used. What mattered was that recruiters and human resource managers used LinkedIn to check out a person's background.

> ☝ Act as if every social media profile is your professional profile.
> Only a fool would believe that a recruiter who stumbles upon a
> crappy Facebook profile is going to think, *Oh, he's using this for
> personal stuff. I'll go find the one he uses for career and professional
> purposes.*
>
> Even if you are "buying" and not "selling," you'll be a better
> negotiator if you can understand and empathize with the posi-
> tion of others.

Other People's Shoes

Speaking of empathy . . . Nate is dyslexic. If you're not familiar with
the condition, here is a description of people with dyslexia from Dr.
Astrid Kopp-Duller in 1995:

> *A dyslexic person of good or average intelligence perceives his en-
> vironment in a different way, and his attention diminishes when
> confronted by letters or numbers. Due to a deficiency in his partial
> performances, his perception of these symbols differs from that by
> non-dyslexic people. This results in difficulties when learning to
> read, write, and do arithmetic.*

I cried after the meeting because it was the first time I understood what it was like to have dyslexia.

Nate's school conducted open houses during which parents could go through exercises that simulated dyslexia. One exercise, for example, involved reading text that was reversed by a mirror. I couldn't complete any of the exercises—not even close. I cried after the meeting because it was the first time I understood what it was like to have dyslexia. The issue was not a lack of intelligence, focus, or diligence.

Wisdom

Empathize with others. As the saying goes, walk a mile in the shoes of others before you judge them. If you believe overcoming learning issues like dyslexia is simply a matter of trying harder and focusing more, you're not even close to understanding, much less empathizing.

The flip side also applies: if someone isn't supportive, perhaps the person isn't evil, bad, or uncaring. Maybe this person simply doesn't know what you're going through, and you should help them walk a mile in your shoes. The open house at Nate's school was one of the most powerful experiences of my life.

Daughters Rule

If daughters can wrap their dads around their little fingers, I'm wound up so tight I can barely breathe. My daughter, Nohemi, has a way of getting to what's important. Some examples:

- "Let's go to the mall," I said to Nate (age ten at the time) and Nohemi (age fourteen at the time) while we were out driving one day. Nate responded, "I've got my wallet." Nohemi trumped him with, "I've got Dad."

- After traveling nonstop for two weeks, I told Nohemi that I wasn't going out of town for the next three. I expected, "That's great, Dad. I miss you when you travel so much." Instead she lamented, "If you don't travel, how will we make money?"
- Audi once loaned me an R8 to test-drive. If you're not a car enthusiast, this is Audi's top-of-the-line sports car, which competes with Porsche, Ferrari, Mercedes, and Lamborghini. I took Nohemi to get ice cream with it, and I warned her, "Don't drop the cone in the car, because Audi will be pissed."

Her response was, "Audi? Who's Audi? Is that like my belly button?"

Her response was, "Audi? Who's Audi? Is that like my belly button?"

Nohemi sitting in the "Outie" R8.

- When Nohemi was eight, she loved online role-playing games. One of them allowed in-game purchases of flowers, treasures, and special powers. Nohemi, using my Apple account, bought $2,500 worth of these digital goods. Her explanation was a deadpan, no-guilt-whatsoever, "I wanted gold coins and special powers." Many other kids must have been doing the same thing because it was easy to reverse the charges.
- Nohemi once called the police when I didn't stop working fast enough to watch television with her. I had a lot of explaining to do to the police dispatcher. Good news: our instructions to call 911 if there was an emergency had sunk in. Bad news: we hadn't properly defined what an emergency was.

Wisdom

Embrace the fact that daughters control how happy their fathers can be. That's all you need to know about raising them.

What I Learned by Almost Drowning

In 1964, a Queens woman named Kitty Genovese was murdered outside of her apartment. According to the early news reports of her death, thirty-seven or more people heard or may have witnessed her killing and did nothing to stop it. This incident led to the development of the social psychology concept called the "bystander effect," which holds that no one takes an action, such as calling the police, because people assume someone else already did.

> **We knew enough to swim parallel to the shore to get out of the riptide, but it's hard to remember what to do when floating facedown all the way to Hawaii is a possible outcome.**

Subsequent analysis showed that there may have been other factors at work, including that none of the witnesses had seen the entirety of the attack on Genovese. Many later stated they thought they were overhearing a lovers' quarrel or drunks leaving a bar.

It seems that the story is more fable than fact, but I had an experience that made the bystander effect real enough for me. In the summer of 2003, I was bodyboarding with my son Nic at Pajaro Dunes in Watsonville, California, and we were sucked away from the shore by a riptide.

We knew enough to swim parallel to the shore to get out of the riptide, but it's hard to remember what to do when floating facedown all the way to Hawaii is a possible outcome. Before we swam to safety, I screamed for help to several people who were walking or jogging along the sand nearby.

One jogger looked around to see if we were yelling at him, saw no one else, and yet kept running—God forbid he didn't get his 10,000 steps in that day. This wasn't the bystander effect, because there were no bystanders around who he could assume were helping us.

You might believe that, had you been in his position, you would have stopped jogging and called for help or yelled directions to swim parallel to the shore, but until you're in a similar situation, you don't know how you'll actually respond.

Don't assume that others are helping when you see people in need. The bystander effect is real. My example was extreme: there weren't any bystanders, and yet the jogger ignored my pleas. Imagine if there were more people around. It's better to have too many people helping someone than too few.

If you are in need yourself, call out to specific people and tell them what to do—for example, "You in the yellow shirt, call the lifeguard!"—and hope they are not as stupid as the guy I encountered.

What Goes Around Comes Around

As I mentioned at the beginning of this book, my father loved musical instruments. He played the piano, saxophone, clarinet, and flute, and he started a big band in the tradition of Guy Lombardo.

We had a piano in our house, and I remember my father practicing the same song over and over until I finally told him, "You can't play the piano. Why don't you just give up?"

He was passionate about something and kept trying to get better at it. I wasn't smart enough to recognize and understand his passion. Criticizing him haunted me during my adult life. It was not only mean but disrespectful.

You'll learn about my own passion for surfing in the next chapter. I was lousy at "reading" waves—meaning knowing when to wait for the right wave and when to start paddling. Nohemi is a very good surfer, and I've asked her for advice many times. But all she would tell me was that I sucked at reading waves, and that over time I was getting worse, not better. This hurt me—as I hurt my father with my comment about his piano playing. I hope she reads this section of the book.

Wisdom

- Don't mistreat others, because you'll be mistreated, too. As the saying goes, "What goes around comes around."

- Prepare for the reality that no one can hurt you as much as someone you love.

- Take up surfing before you're sixty-two years old—and you're about to learn more about surfing than you ever wanted to in the next chapter.

08

Sports

*The heaviness of being successful was replaced by
the lightness of being a beginner again.*

—Steve Jobs

From the seventh grade on, I loved sports. Along the way to old age, I
played football, soccer, basketball, tennis, and hockey, and then I took
up surfing. I'm not a "natural athlete," so none of these sports came
easy to me. But what I lack in ability, I made up for in determination—
which is, come to think of it, the story of my life in general.

It's Never Too Late

For me there were only two seasons in high school: training for football
and playing football. It's hard to explain the exhilaration of hitting

someone without coming off as a psychopath, but the feeling is there and explains why the sport is so popular despite its danger.

I loved my football coaches, Edward Hamada, Charlie Kaaihue, and Joseph Yelas. On and off the field they taught me the value of hard work and teamwork. My two oldest boys had a similar experience with their coaches, Pete Lavorato and Mark Modeste, at Sacred Heart Prep in Atherton.

As I mentioned earlier, I almost picked a college based on where I could play football, but my father put the kibosh on that. When I started at Stanford, like a fool I tried out for the football team. However, after two days (really one practice), it was obvious that Pac-12 (it was Pac-10 back then) college football was a different game in which everyone was bigger, faster, and stronger than me.

Since college, I've gone from one sport to another in streaks. First it was tennis. Then it was basketball. At forty-eight, I took up hockey after I attended my first hockey game in 2002. It was a San Jose Sharks game, and the occasion was the birthday of a friend named Marc Rogers. My wife and I brought Nic and Noah, who were nine and seven years old, respectively, at the time.

My sons loved the game. The hitting and nonstop action appealed to their all-boy brains, so they told us that they wanted to play hockey. Being Silicon Valley parents, we dared not deprive our precious jewels of pursuing anything, so we embraced the sport with great enthusiasm.

Early on Beth said something that changed my life: "I don't want you to be a typical Silicon Valley father who's on the sideline, tapping away on a BlackBerry, and looking up at the game every once in a while. I want you involved in their lives, so you should take up hockey, too."

I always listen to my wife, so I took up hockey forty-four years later than every Canadian does. You know I'm from Hawaii, and there isn't a lot of pond hockey there. In fact, the primary use of ice in Hawaii was to make shave-ice cones.

Thus, I had never skated on ice (or any other surface) when I started. I didn't even know that you had to sharpen skates before using them. The first time I stepped onto the ice, with sharpened skates and padded up, was a religious experience. I was hooked in the first ten feet, and hockey became an obsession.

If I was not on the road, I played almost every day—sometimes twice a day. I have taken my hockey equipment when I travel and played in Doha, Honolulu, Vancouver, Toronto, Charlotte, Austin, and Minneapolis. Before a trip to Bratislava, Slovakia, I told the hosts that I'd love to play hockey while I was there.

The next thing that I knew, the hosts had arranged for a game with twenty-two local players including Peter Stastny, the second-highest NHL scorer of the 1980s and a member of the Hockey Hall of Fame.

The game was at the Ondrej Nepela Arena, which seats 10,000 people—not quite the neighborhood rinks I was used to. (There were roughly 9,990 empty seats that day.) My hosts also provided jerseys for both teams, as well as bags, sticks, gloves, pads, helmets, and pants for the players who didn't have equipment.

On the last play of the game, I got a pass from Stastny and took a wrist shot. I thought the goalie stopped the puck, but Stastny said that I scored. Who am I to argue with someone who's in the Hockey Hall of Fame?

While I was on a speaking trip to Toronto in January 2014, the hosts of the event rented the rink at Ryerson University and invited a few local players, plus a guy named Eric Lindros.

You may have heard of Eric: he played for the Philadelphia Flyers, Toronto Maple Leafs, New York Rangers, and Dallas Stars and was

Playing hockey in Slovenia.

inducted into the Hockey Hall of Fame in 2016. I played on Eric's line. He fed me passes for one hour, but I never scored.

Another hockey story involves Bret Hedican of the Carolina Hurricanes and Anaheim Ducks. I met him through his wife, Kristi Yama-

Hanging with Eric Lindros.

guchi, the Olympic figure skater. Kristi and I had met through mutual friends from Hawaii.

At my invitation, Bret once broke down and played on a tournament team that I put together. Let's just say that the other players in the tournament thought it was unfair that an ex-NHL player was on our side.

My response was, "When you go to work on Monday, would you rather tell your friends that you played against NHLer and Olympian Bret Hedican, or against a bunch of losers like the rest of us?"

In my mind, I did them a great favor.

Wisdom

Keep trying new stuff. It's never too late to acquire a new skill or improve a current one. The acquisition of skill is a process, not an event, and the process itself can be the reward.

When you pursue something passionately, if not obsessively, it makes you a more interesting person. My love of hockey helped me make friends far beyond the tech community of Silicon Valley, and those relationships enriched my life.

Life Regresses to the Mean

One last hockey story. An injury to my eye in 2015 required that I not wear contact lenses for several weeks, so I played with glasses. The first time that I did so, I also drank a Jamaica Blue Mountain coffee from Philz—a $10 cup of joe.

That day I scored six goals. A day later I played again, and I scored another six goals. The time after that, four goals. Then I played in a high-level game where I was the worst player and scored two goals. I had never scored as many goals before (and never would again).

I understand superstition. For example, rumor has it that Michael Jordan wore the same North Carolina shorts under his Chicago Bulls shorts for his entire career. There may have been causative reasons for my scoring streak:

- Caffeine improved my athletic performance.
- Glasses provided better vision than contacts.
- Glasses provided worse vision and fogged up so I had to compensate by focusing more on the puck.
- There were lousy goalies for those games.

Shortly after this, even wearing glasses, I went back to seldom scoring. Scientists call this "regressing to the mean"—that is, returning to my average level of play. But the scoring streak sure was fun while it lasted.

> ## *Wisdom*
>
> Don't get too cocky when things are good, or too negative when things are bad. Life regresses to the mean over the long run. The wisdom is to keep working at it in order to raise the mean.

Even Later, It's Never Too Late

In the summer of 2015, at the age of sixty-one, I tried paddleboarding at the University of California at Santa Barbara family summer camp.

I must have a Jesus complex—that is, the desire to "walk on water" whether it is solid (hockey) or liquid (surfing).

I liked paddleboarding because it strengthened my core muscles and improved my balance—both of which are good for hockey. At that time, every physical activity was to improve my hockey proficiency.

That fall I went to Hawaii for a speech and took paddleboard lessons from a legendary Hawaiian waterman named Kainoa McGee. At this point, I was happy inside the reef of Ala Moana beach. Paddleboarding for me was about cruising around on calm waters, not catching waves.

A few months later I tried prone surfing in Hawaii—again, McGee was my instructor. During two hours of instruction, I stood up for a total of thirty seconds, and this was with McGee pushing me into the waves. It was a pathetic performance.

(If you are unfamiliar with surfing terminology, paddle surfing involves catching waves on a stand-up paddleboard, or SUP. You stand on the board the whole time—at least until you fall off. Prone surfing is what most people are familiar with, where you lie on a surfboard, catch a wave, and pop up to a standing position.)

The following summer, surfing became a passion for my daughter. After my experiences in Hawaii, I thought that prone surfing was too difficult, but I decided to transcend *supporting* her interest to *sharing* it. Since I couldn't prone surf, I decided to at least learn how to paddle surf. If I took up hockey for Nic and Noah, I should take up surfing for Nohemi.

Later that year a friend named Mike Ahern offered to introduce me to Jeff Clark. I was into paddle surfing for only a few months at that point, so I didn't know who Clark was. When I told Nohemi that we could meet Clark, she jumped out of her skin with excitement.

I learned that Clark is the person who discovered Mavericks, the big-wave (as in, sixty feet high) surfing location near Half Moon Bay in Northern California. He surfed Mavericks by himself for fifteen years before anyone else tried it. Suffice it to say, he's one of the most famous surfers and board makers in the world.

In February 2017, Clark took Ahern, Nohemi, Nate, and me on a tour of Mavericks. The next day, by chance, Clark was in Santa Cruz visiting a friend who lived a block from our beach house. (I knew it was him only because I recognized his Mercedes-Benz Sprinter van.)

Later that day I tried to prone surf, but I couldn't catch a wave, so I gave up. I went back to my house, ate, rested, and decided to go back into the water to paddle surf. I did this for an hour and caught several waves.

At the end of the session, I climbed the stairs at 38th Avenue at Pleasure Point and saw three people sitting on the bench laughing up a storm. To my horror, it was Nohemi; her surf coach, Calder Nold; and Clark. They had been watching me the entire time. Clark, discoverer of Mavericks, had watched me surf two-foot waves.

He told me I was trying to catch waves correctly, but that my board had the wrong kind of rails (the outside edge). Right then and there, I asked Clark to make me a paddleboard. When a legend has seen you in action and tells you what equipment you need, it's meant to be.

I visited my board as it was being glassed and painted in Coronado, California, in March 2017. A few weeks later, I picked it up at Clark's shop in Half Moon Bay. A few days after that, he and I went out paddle surfing at a break called Second Peak at Pleasure Point.

I won't die. Jeff will save me.

I was demolished by the first wave I tried to catch. As I was tumbled around in the surf, I thought, *I won't die. Jeff will save me.* When I finally got to the surface, Clark said, "Your two legs were out of the water, and you were kicking, so you were driving yourself deeper, but I knew you'd be okay."

If you've learned nothing else about me, you know that I don't give up easily, so I kept paddle surfing with the Clark board. In April 2017, I took it with me to Hawaii for a week during my kids' spring break. Again, I took lessons from McGee.

If you surfed at Pleasure Point from May to July 2017 and saw a kook surping on a paddleboard, it was me.

I expected him to say, "Your dumb *haole* friend made you the wrong board," but to my great relief, he told me it was perfect for me. With McGee's help, I got to the point where I was catching waves that would have crushed me a few weeks earlier.

At the end of one session, I asked him what he thought of me prone surfing, instead of paddle surfing, with the board. He said it would be a good idea, as it would help me become "one" with the board, so I threw him my paddle and he started pushing me into waves.

To my (and McGee's) amazement, I caught the next four waves, and fell in love with prone surfing on a paddleboard. Remember that prior to this day, I had never succeeded at prone surfing with a regular surfboard for more than a few seconds at a time, and only after someone pushed me into a wave.

That's the day that I hung up my paddle and focused on "surping"—surfing + SUP-ing (stand-up paddleboarding). To surfing cognoscenti, this is "kooky" (something a clueless beginner would do), because surfers use boards that are approximately 20 to 50 percent smaller than a paddleboard. However, I needed a big, stable board because my balance sucked.

After I returned to California, Microsoft asked me to make a presentation. In addition to my exorbitant fee, I asked for a board to see how much the company really wanted me. A few weeks later, I received a high-performance paddleboard designed by Dave Kalama, another legendary Hawaiian surfer.

Surping on the Dave Kalama board.

For months, Nold had been telling me to stop paddle surfing, man up, and take up prone surfing. So I began a quest to learn how to prone surf by surping on the paddleboard. After a few weeks, I got an even smaller Dave Kalama board. Nold took me on as a student despite (1) my age and (2) my theory of using a small paddleboard as a surfboard. As he said, "I could teach you to surf on a piece of Styrofoam if you wanted me to."

My part of the deal with Nold was to practice and work my ass off—not just show up on weekends and expect to become a good surfer. For example, I practiced "popping up" from a prone position to the

standing position at least thirty times a day, and I did exercises on a balance board made by a company called Indo Board.

If you surfed at Pleasure Point from May to July 2017 and saw a kook surping on a paddleboard, it was me. You might have thought it was strange or stupid to surf with a paddleboard, but it enabled me to (1) learn how to prone surf and (2) fall in love with prone surfing.

And "fall in love" is not an exaggeration. I surfed twice a day for most of the summer of 2017. It was my "endless summer." On some days, all four of my kids were out there with me, and these were some of the most precious moments of my life.

Surfing with Nohemi.

In November 2017, Nold convinced me to buy a custom-made surfboard from Bob Pearson of Pearson Arrow. Pearson is a legendary shaper for the best surfers in the world. After ninety minutes of interrogation and therapy, Pearson decided on a board based on my skill level and the kind of waves I'd ride.

Bob shaping Moby Dick 1. Left to right: Bob Pearson, Calder Nold, and me.

This board changed my life. I named it Moby Dick 1, because it was big and white. There's usually a trade-off with surfboards between speed, stability, and maneuverability, but Pearson made one for me that embodied all three. It truly changed my life.

Wisdom

My surfing saga taught me six lessons:

👍 Follow the lead of your kids. Kids often adopt the passions of their parents. For example, if their parents surf, the kids will follow. I did the opposite: taking up what my kids loved. This is a better way to go, because kids don't feel pressured into embracing the passions of their parents. They will never have to "fill the shoes" of their parents since their parents will never be better than they are, and their parents are less likely to try to coach them, because they know less than their kids.

Grind it out. If you're going to follow your kids, you have to dedicate a great deal of time and effort to doing so, since you're starting late. My path to surfing competency was the same as my path to speaking, writing, and evangelizing: grit, repetition, and hard work, not "natural talent." As I've said, there are plenty of people who are more talented than me and plenty of people who work harder than me, but very few people who are both.

Ignore the naysayers and critics. If people tell you that you're too anything (old, dumb, short, whatever) to succeed, ignore them. They might be right, but they might be wrong, too. There's only one way to find out: try it. This applies to the naysayer and critic inside of you—self-doubt is a bitch. Remember to read Brenda Ueland's *If You Want to Write*!

Don't be afraid to go "outside the box." I reasoned that I needed the stability of a paddleboard and the maneuverability of a surfboard to hone my skills. Solution: using a high-performance paddleboard as a low-performance surfboard. Even Nold reluctantly came to admit that this was an effective transition strategy.

Get the right equipment. There's a theory that if you're good enough, the equipment doesn't matter—along the lines of "It's the photographer, not the camera." This is fine if you're young, poor, and flexible. But if you're old, rich, and stiff, you should use every means to succeed.

> Find the right coach or two. There's no way I would have achieved my prone surfing competency without Nold and McGee. In other words, work hard but also work smart by finding people who can help you. When you start at sixty-two, you don't have time to figure things out by yourself.

The Coolest People Use Apple Stuff

In August 2016, I was in the Apple store on State Street in Santa Barbara for Nate's monthly repair of his iPhone screen. A guy came up to me and asked, "Are you Hawaiian?"

I responded, "No, I'm Japanese."

Then he said, "You look like Guy Kawasaki."

I responded, "I *am* Guy Kawasaki, but I'm not Hawaiian."

He introduced himself as Shaun Tomson, and the name meant nothing to me. But the Apple genius helping me asked, "Are you *the* Shaun Tomson?"

The Shaun Tomson answered in the affirmative. The Apple genius filled me in by telling me that Shaun had been a world champion surfer in the 1970s and 1980s and was one of the most famous surfers in the world.

Okay, then! Tomson and I talked, and I explained how I had tried surfing a year ago and that my two youngest children loved it. He volunteered to take us surfing while we were in Santa Barbara.

A few days later, it happened. However, even with the help of one of the greatest surfers in the world, I could not stand up on the board. Shaun said it was because the waves were too small, but I knew he was being kind.

He also said that, according to surfing rules, if your hands leave the rails and you make a movement to stand, that counts as a ride. By his count, I had four rides. But really, it was zero.

Hanging with Shaun Tomson.

Wisdom

Talk to strangers and buy stuff at Apple stores. You can meet the coolest people there. If you want to meet me by chance, I shop at the Apple store on University Avenue in Palo Alto.

Learn to look on the bright side. In this case, if Nate had not cracked his iPhone case, I would not have become friends with Shaun Tomson.

An even better way to meet me, though, is to surf at the 38th Avenue break in Santa Cruz. I am there almost every weekend. Just look for the guy who looks like Jackie Chan on a big, white board.

Tomson and I became good friends. He has helped me with my surfing, and I have helped him with his writing and speaking. The wisdom in his "surfer's code" is great, too:

1. I will never turn my back on the ocean: Passion
2. I will paddle around the impact zone: No shortcuts
3. I will take the drop with commitment: Courage, focus, and determination
4. I will never fight a riptide: The danger of pride and egotism
5. I will always paddle back out: Perseverance in the face of challenges
6. I will watch out for other surfers after a big set: Responsibility
7. I will know that there will always be another wave: Optimism
8. I will ride and not paddle into shore: Self-esteem
9. I will pass on my stoke to a non-surfer: Sharing knowledge and giving back
10. I will catch a wave every day, even in my mind: Imagination
11. I will realize that all surfers are joined by one ocean: Empathy
12. I will honor the sport of kings: Honor and integrity

One Last Surfing Story

In July 2018, Nold, now our entire family's surfing coach, had a talk with Nohemi and Nate. A few people who surf where we do had complained to him that my kids were catching too many waves. They asked him to tell Nohemi and Nate to catch fewer waves.

Three questions immediately came to mind: First, was it my kids' fault that they are good? Second, was it Nold's fault that he coached them so well that they got good? Third, was it my kids' or Nold's fault that the complainers couldn't catch as many waves?

That said, there is a code and etiquette that people share waves and don't take too many. You are supposed to catch a wave and then wait your turn for the next wave, so Nold did talk to my kids.

Wisdom

🤙 Pay attention to the rules—even if they are unwritten and lead to catching fewer waves. That's how this story applies to my kids. But there's also a lesson for the complainers . . .

🤙 Get better—sit in the right place, paddle harder, and use the right kind of surfboard instead of complaining that two kids are getting more waves than you.

Honestly, if my kids complained to Nold that they weren't getting enough waves, we would tell them to suck it up and get better, because it's a cruel world.

By the way, I also asked Nold if anyone had complained that *I* caught too many waves, and his answer was, "No, no one mentioned you"—which sorely disappointed me. And thus it became a goal of mine that I would become so proficient at catching waves that people would complain about me to Nold.

09

LOL

[A] quotation is a handy thing to have about, saving one the trouble of thinking for oneself, always a laborious business.

—A. A. Milne

In this book, LOL stands for Laugh-Out Lessons. These are the funny things that happened to me—or that I caused. There is humor in these stories, but they also embody interesting, and important, life lessons.

Simplest Is Best

Here are three anecdotes that illustrate the concept that simplest is best.

(1) In 2016, I was on the board of trustees of the Wikimedia Foundation, and I attended the Wikimania conference in Esino Lario, Italy.

(Wikimania is the annual meeting for worldwide members of the Wikipedia community.)

Some participants came from countries where the government frowns upon, if not prevents, the free flow of information. Thus, they did not want to be photographed and were able to use a special fluorescent green lanyard to hold their badge to signal this desire.

> "I picked the green lanyard because it matches my earrings better."

I saw a woman from a country whose government was in a state of flux wearing one of these lanyards. Later I overheard her say, "I picked the green lanyard because it matches my earrings better." So much for the assumption that it was a personal safety concern over the fear of government reprisal.

(2) Heidi Roizen is a big-deal venture capitalist and tech guru in Silicon Valley who's been a friend of mine since 1983. Her father gave her a hard time about driving an expensive BMW. One night she took him to MacArthur Park, a restaurant in Menlo Park.

When they came out of the restaurant after dinner, her car was still in front where she had parked it. She told her father, "Do you see why I drive an expensive car? They leave it out front, and this means we don't have to wait for the valet to get it."

A second later, a pissed-off valet came up to her and told her that because she had taken her keys with her, no one had been able to move her car all night.

(3) In September 2017, I received an unexpected Amazon shipment of wart-removal medicine. When I asked Beth about it, she said that she hadn't ordered it, either, but that she had been doing online research about wart removal. Could it be that someone had hacked her

computer, figured out she was looking at wart medicine, found our address, and ordered it for us? That was scary—though nonsensical. Hackers don't order medicine for you.

The next day, I went through the trash and found the box the shipment had come in and saw that it was ordered by someone else named Guy who lived on the same street. No hacking was involved.

Wisdom

Start with the simplest explanation. It's often the best—this principle is otherwise known as Occam's Razor. For example, a badge to match the color of your earrings, a valet who needs your keys to move your car, and an incorrect delivery were all the simplest explanations.

Sinister plots, hacking, and conspiracies are seldom responsible. Stupidity and luck—good or bad—are usually the most likely reasons that something happened, so don't think too much and don't be paranoid.

Showing Weakness Is a Sign of Strength

Zatoichi was the name of a blind masseur in a series of Japanese movies. He wandered the countryside minding his own business, but he inevitably wound up righting wrongs with his sword. (Think: blind Japanese Robin Hood.)

I saw many Zatoichi movies when I was growing up in Hawaii. This was before the movie industry was concerned about damaging minors with violence and gore, and I guess my parents reasoned that samurai films were part of our culture.

I survived the cinematic trauma and even learned a valuable lesson. In one movie, as I recall, a criminal gang captured Zatoichi, and the boss of the gang forced him to have sex with a prostitute in front of him and his henchman at a Japanese inn.

The gang members consider Zatoichi to be weak because he agreed to this humiliation, and they laugh their heads off (literally). Then the innkeeper points out that it's difficult for a man to have sex if he's scared—in other words, Zatoichi wasn't scared, so they should be. Shortly after, Zatoichi killed them all.

Fast-forward to June 11, 2007. Another samurai, by the name of Steve Jobs, proclaimed at the introduction of the iPhone, "Our innovative approach, using Web 2.0–based standards, lets developers create amazing new applications while keeping the iPhone secure and reliable."

In May 2008, the samurai's company issued a press release with this headline: "Apple Executives to Showcase Mac OS X Leopard and OS X iPhone Development Platforms at WWDC 2008 Keynote."

Let me translate these statements. The first meant that iPhone was a closed system; developers could not create stand-alone apps for it. All they could do was write plug-ins to add functionality via Safari, Apple's browser on the phone.

The second statement was a complete reversal of the first. Now Apple was permitting and even encouraging stand-alone iPhone apps. Developers went on to create hundreds of thousands of them, and it was these apps that were crucial to the ultimate success of the iPhone.

While Apple's statements are not as dramatic as sex and decapitations, they illustrate the same concept: strong people can show weakness. Zatoichi was forced to have sex in front of the hoodlums. Steve Jobs had to reverse his position on the closed architecture of the iPhone.

Wisdom

Don't be afraid to show weakness. Strong people can admit a mistake, change their minds, and tolerate humiliation. Often this is the first step toward building strength.

Weak people are afraid to show vulnerability. They think this gives their competition the advantage or positions them poorly. Strong people don't see it this way.

When you encounter weakness, flexibility, or the willingness to compromise, don't underestimate your competition and don't overestimate yourself.

When you encounter what appears to be strength, don't overestimate your competition and don't underestimate yourself. In short, be kind, flexible, and humble when you are in a position of strength. This communicates true power better than brute force does.

> ## . . . be kind, flexible, and humble when you are in a position of strength. This communicates true power . . .

I'm a Lucky Guy

The scariest experience of my life was visiting San Quentin State Prison. This facility is located north of San Francisco, just across the Golden Gate Bridge. The complex is on 432 acres, and it housed approximately three thousand inmates at the time of my trips there. It also operated the only death row for men in California.

I visited San Quentin in 2009 and 2011. Before you think that I'm a recidivist criminal, the reason for my presence there was to support an organization called The Last Mile, whose mission is to prepare prisoners for a successful reentry into society.

Left to right: Robert Scoble and Dave Winer, outside of San Quentin.
Surely I could have outrun these two guys.

The process of visiting San Quentin is complicated. You cannot wear jeans or some specific colors of clothing because of their associations with certain gangs. And you must agree to the state of California's no-hostage-exchange policy—to quote our guide:

> *The State of California, Department of Corrections, does not recognize releasing you for the release of a hostage. However, we will do everything humanly possible to obtain your release and make sure that you're safe.*

My first visit was with a group of bloggers. We went through the guard station and entered a courtyard next to the solitary-confinement building. It was a fine fall day; so far so good. Then I walked down a ramp, turned the corner, and saw the prison yard. Holy shit, the scene took my breath away.

All the movies and HBO specials I'd watched hadn't prepared me for the reality of the prison yard. The inmates, grouped by race, were lifting weights, playing basketball, and playing tennis. They outnumbered the guards by dozens—and the few guards with rifles posted at the top of the wall weren't that reassuring.

> "I may not be faster than these prisoners, but I know I'm faster than you two white boys."

I was near Robert Scoble and Dave Winer, two guys who were considered, and considered themselves, the badasses of tech. But we were all snowflakes in that setting. One thing was reassuring: I was in better physical condition than Scoble and Winer, so I told them, "I may not be faster than these prisoners, but I know I'm faster than you two white boys."

Then we went into a cell block where dozens of prisoners were hanging around outside cells. Suddenly I remembered the no-hostage policy. Holy shit again. Next, we visited the cafeteria and then had a tour of the defunct gas chamber (California switched to lethal injection in 1994).

Fast-forward to my second visit to San Quentin, when I taught a class on influence and persuasion using my book *Enchantment*. My audience was intelligent, respectful, and motivated. And these guys were murderers and other kinds of felons—not white-collar criminals who bounced a few checks or traded inside stock information.

Somebody Will Always Find a Problem

I attended the 2016 Consumer Electronics Show in Las Vegas and test-drove a car that wasn't available in the United States.

For the show, the cars were disguised in a vinyl skin with the letters *C*, *E*, and *S* positioned in various rotations and orders. (Manufacturers cover cars in this manner to make it difficult for people to get a good idea about the final exterior design.)

I created a video of the exterior of the car and posted the video on my social media accounts. On Facebook I saw two comments to the effect of, "Why did the manufacturer print 'Jew Suc' on its cars?" I had no idea what these comments referred to and asked for an explanation.

To my amazement, these people had seen places in the video where it looked like the words "Jew Suc" were written because of how the

Do you see the offensive phrase on this car?

letters *C*, *E*, and *S* were displayed. Think about this. For people to make this observation, two things had to occur.

First, on the top row, the *C* had to be rotated 180 degrees to look like a *J*, and the *E* had to be rotated 270 degrees to look like a *W*. On the second row, the *C* had to be rotated 270 degrees to look like a *U*. Second, people had to notice this as a video was playing—as opposed to seeing a static picture. They thought the car manufacturer had intentionally printed "Jew Suc" because of an anti-Semitic attitude.

Knock me over with a feather. Perhaps someone at the car company could have looked at the vinyl wrap to check for offensive phrases, but that would not have occurred to me. Nor would it have occurred to me that any car manufacturer would plaster offensive messages on a prototype car. Sadly, some people saw it this way.

Wisdom

Make your best effort and proceed boldly. Some people will see problems and controversies that aren't there. Making everyone happy is impossible.

Try to prevent problems rather than to correct them. In this case, it would have been smart to ask someone with "fresh eyes" to have a look at your efforts. The oft-cited cautionary tale that people use to illustrate this advice is how General Motors named a car "Nova," which did not sell well in Mexico.

The reason for its poor sales was supposedly that *no va* in Spanish means "not going," and people would not buy a car so described. However, Snopes, the online fact-checking site (snopes.com/fact-check/chevrolet-nova-name-spanish), dispels this story:

- *No va* are two words with the accent on the second word, *va*. "Nova" is one word with the accent on the syllable "no." I love this sentence from Snopes: "Assuming that Spanish speakers would naturally see the word 'nova' as equivalent to the phrase '*no va*' and think 'Hey, this car doesn't go!' is akin to assuming that English speakers would spurn a dinette set sold under the name *Notable* because nobody wants a dinette set that doesn't include a table."
- Pemex, the Mexican oil company, sells gasoline called Nova. People wouldn't buy a gasoline that meant "not going," and the folks at Pemex would know better, too.
- When a company introduces a product to a country, many local people work on the manuals, marketing

materials, and advertising. Dealers see the product before introduction. The idea that some stupid gringos from Detroit got off a plane and instantly launched a poorly named car doesn't make sense.

Here's what you can learn from the Nova account: don't believe everything you read or hear. If a story truly matters to you, then check it out. Someone has probably done the fact-checking already.

Externalities Are Deceiving

After quitting law school at UC Davis, I returned to Hawaii, and my father got me a job working for his friend the lieutenant governor of Hawaii, Nelson K. Doi. At the time, Doi was starting the Hawaii Commission on Crime, and my job was to compile information about how other states had set up crime commissions.

Doi was a family friend, and years before, he had invited me to go hunting with him on the Big Island, where he was a judge at the time.

On the day of this safari, he picked me up in a Jeep and was wearing hunting boots, camo pants, and a camo jacket. But he had to perform a wedding first, so we got in the Jeep and went to his office. He put on a robe, married the couple, and then off we went, armed with bows and arrows, to hunt wild goats on an old lava field.

Because of my ineptness, we never got close enough to a goat to bag one, but we stumbled upon a wild boar—or, more accurately, it stumbled upon us and then took off and jumped into a lava hole. As we came up to the hole, Doi nocked an arrow and pulled back the bow.

Then he told me, "See that tree? If the boar attacks us, climb up that tree as fast as you can."

Death by boar gore wasn't on my agenda, and you don't argue with a judge, so I was ready to climb the tree. Doi shot and killed the boar. We hauled it out of the lava hole, gutted it, and took it to the Jeep. He sent me home with wild boar meat—which, by the way, was tough and tasted terrible.

Wisdom

Look beyond the cover. This is true for people as well as books. On that day, Doi was literally judge, jury, and executioner, and I learned not to judge (pun intended) people by their clothes. Under Doi's robes was a hunter, and under the hunting clothes was a judge.

Human tendency is to overestimate the competence/power/ goodness of people who are well dressed and underestimate those qualities for people who are not well dressed.

Perhaps the wise thing to do is consider appearance as only one factor, and a minor one at that, when making judgments.

It's All Relative

In July 2018, I attended the RISE tech conference in Hong Kong in order to shoot a video with the chairman of Mercedes-Benz, Dieter Zetsche, who was giving a keynote speech at the conference.

(Side story: When Zetsche and I sat down to shoot the video in a Chinese restaurant, the table was rocking. He grabbed a piece of paper,

Dieter Zetsche and I at the wobbly table in Hong Kong.

folded it up to the right thickness, and leveled the table. This is the kind of commitment to engineering that you want to see in the chairman of the company that makes your car.)

I was not the only Mercedes-Benz brand ambassador at the event. The company also brought in Mike Horn. He is, in a nutshell, one of the world's greatest adventurers:

- He journeyed around the world at the equator without any motorized transportation.
- He made a solo circumnavigation of the Arctic Circle.
- With a Norwegian explorer, he was the first man to travel to the North Pole during the winter without motorized transport or dogs.

It had been ten months since we had seen each other, so he asked me what I had been doing. My response was: "I've written a book and become a better surfer."

I then made the mistake of asking him what he had been doing, and his response was: "I hiked across Antarctica, sailed from Antarctica to the Philippines, drove from Singapore to Pakistan, climbed an 8,000-meter mountain in Pakistan, sailed from the Philippines to the North Pole, and then walked across the North Pole. And I wrote two books."

Okay, then. It was clear who was the big dog on the porch!

Wisdom

Be humble. We're all specks of dust in the universe, but some specks sure do more than others.

The Fallacy of "Perfect" Information

In July 2011, the intersection of Highway 101 and Highway 405 (northwest of downtown Los Angeles) was closed for the fifty-three hours that it took to demolish an overpass.

Sometimes it's best to go the opposite of the crowd that's going opposite the crowd.

This is such a heavily traveled area that the closure was nicknamed "carpocalypse" and "carmageddon" with predictions of massive traffic jams and delays. Government officials warned people to stay at home and avoid driving unless necessary.

The warnings scared people away from the area. I could not avoid it because I was driving from Anaheim to Northern California, and to my surprise there was no traffic at that intersection. Zero. Nada. I flew in at sixty-five miles per hour. It was probably the best day to drive through that area in the history of Los Angeles.

Crowdsourced traffic information on a service such as Waze provides a way to test the fallacy of perfect information. Waze routes you through traffic based on the speed of other cars traveling in the same area. If it sees that the highway is crowded, it will reroute you onto side streets.

However, I swear that sometimes there are so many Waze users in a particular area that too many people are rerouted—making the Waze-optimized path worse than the original one. Sometimes it's best to go the opposite of the crowd that's going opposite the crowd.

Wisdom

Don't assume that "perfect information" is perfect. Maybe a double fake is better—that is, since so many people are operating on what they think is perfect information, the way to go is against it.

The lesson here isn't to ignore safety warnings and recommendations, but when you're not facing a life-and-death decision, see what happens if you "think different," as Apple's advertising advised.

You Never Know

A short time after Yahoo! started in 1995, venture capitalist and start-up empire-maker Michael Moritz asked me if I wanted to apply for the

CEO position. He was on Yahoo!'s board of directors as a representative of Sequoia Capital, one of the company's lead investors.

At the time, my wife, Beth, our son Nic, and I lived in San Francisco on Union Street in a house with well-trimmed bougainvillea, and Yahoo!'s offices were an hour's drive away in light traffic. My wife was also in beta with our second son, Noah, so we were about to have a two-year-old and a newborn.

I told Moritz that I didn't want to interview for the job because it meant two hours of driving every day, and I couldn't see how the company could make money. Yahoo! was then nothing more than a collection of the cofounders' favorite websites.

FYI, over the course of its operation, Sequoia's investments had achieved a public-market value of $1.4 trillion, so turning down this interview was foolish—at least in hindsight. This was the costliest mistake I've made in my career. As I'm writing this book, I've revisited this decision for approximately nineteen years, thirty days, eight hours, and fifteen minutes. Here's how I look at it:

- If I had interviewed, I probably would have gotten the job.
- My stock option package would have amounted to 5 percent of the company.
- Yahoo!'s market capitalization peaked at $100 billion in the 2000 time frame.
- Five percent of $100 billion is $5 billion.

Let's say my calculation is off by 50 percent. This still means I lost $2.5 billion. And $2.5 billion here and $2.5 billion there adds up to real money. The question I've been asking myself ever since is, *Why was I so stupid?*

I rationalize (while simultaneously congratulating myself) that I picked my family over money. What price can you put on being around when your kids are growing up?

I have no regrets about choosing to spend time with my wife and kids, but what pisses me off about my decision is that:

- I thought the internet was nothing more than an extension of personal computers—it was simply what was coming through the Macintosh modem cable. It wasn't a new industry.
- I didn't even meet with a world-famous venture capitalist from a world-famous firm after he asked me if I was interested in a job.
- I wasn't smart enough to understand that companies morph. Yahoo! may have started as a directory of the internet, but it morphed into email, commerce, search, photography, and so much more.

After this experience, whenever I heard a "stupid" idea for a company, I always thought back to my Yahoo! debacle—truly, "you never know." Over the course of several decades of living in Silicon Valley, I saw some other "dumb" ideas do quite well.

- The world didn't need another search engine when Google started in 1996, because there was already Excite, Infoseek, AltaVista, Yahoo!, Lycos, LookSmart, and Inktomi.
- YouTube required infinite bandwidth and infinite storage for uploading illegal video. Its tipping point occurred when people made their own videos of what happens when you drop Mentos into Diet Coke.

- If you were the buyer of a used HP printer on eBay, you didn't know if it would work. If you were the seller of a used HP printer, you didn't know if you would get paid. Besides this, what could go wrong with an online marketplace?

The other large mistakes I made were leaving Apple twice and turning down Steve's offer to run Apple University a few years after I left the second time.

These Apple mistakes weren't as costly as declining the Yahoo! interview. However, if I had stayed either time, I would surf every day instead of only on weekends. That said, I probably would have become an insufferable asshole, because inhaling the same fumes for a few decades can do that to you.

Wisdom

At the cost of $2.5 billion, I damn well better have gained some wisdom. You be the judge of whether these lessons are worth it:

Suspend disbelief. "Silly" ideas like Yahoo! can succeed if they're riding a tsunami. A rising tide floats all boats. Doomed companies like Apple can roar back.

Meet with a venture capitalist from the firm that funded companies whose total value exceeded $1.4 trillion (including, for example, Apple, Cisco, and Atari). My lack of pattern recognition was pathetic.

Never bet against, nor lose faith in, someone like Steve Jobs. For example, I advise against betting against Elon Musk.

Everyone Does Stupid Things

Here are stories of things I've done that make me look back and ask myself, *What was I thinking? I could have killed someone!*

- When Nic was a baby, he was fussy—crying all the time no matter what we did. I would often swaddle him tightly in a blanket so that he would fall asleep. I still have nightmares that this could have caused him to overheat or asphyxiate.

- Once I could not get a blender blade to spin, so I took off the top and turned it on to see what the problem was. The manufacturer was smart enough to know that people are dumb enough to do this and ensure that the blades don't fly out, but I still have nightmares of the blade flying out and decapitating me.

- I noticed that dropping dry ice into water creates a lot of gas. What, I wondered, would happen if you added dry ice to water in a plastic water bottle and sealed the bottle? Nate and I decided to conduct an experiment in our backyard to find out, and we both learned a valuable lesson in the process. After a short time, the bottle exploded—luckily, not near us. Nate did some research and learned that this is called a dry-ice bomb, which is as dangerous as it sounds. Do not experiment with dry ice. I still have nightmares of Nate or me being blown up.

Wisdom

Be skeptical of experts, because everyone does stupid things from time to time. An expert in one field is not necessarily an expert in another. For example, a brain surgeon might not be the best person to run a government agency.

Also, someone who isn't an expert in one field might be an expert in another. For example, that old guy who can barely surf might be an expert in entrepreneurship and evangelism.

After many false positives and false negatives, I adopted the strategy of being skeptical of everyone, but I also assume that everyone can do something better. This combination of perspectives has worked well for me.

10

Skills

Writing isn't about making money, getting famous, getting dates, getting laid, or making friends. In the end, it's about enriching the lives of those who will read your work, and enriching your own life, as well.

—Stephen King

What you've read so far in this book are the inside stories of the skills I acquired in evangelism, writing, public speaking, and social media. It took me approximately thirty-five years to amass this wisdom. FYI, I didn't have a master plan or cogent strategy to do so. I acquired these skills by diving in and learning by doing. I hope that I can help you shorten your learning curve.

Evangelism

In 1983, Mike Boich and I began to travel across the United States with two Mac prototypes in a bag and a stack of nondisclosure agreements. We met with companies with thousands of employees as well as "two guys in a garage."

We were the Macintosh Division's evangelists. Our job title, "evangelist," was a derivative of a Greek word meaning "bringing the good news." Our good news was that the Mac would make people more creative and productive.

When Boich and I evangelized software and hardware companies, our pitch stressed three reasons to create Macintosh products:

- Macintosh was the computer for "the rest of us"—that is, the people who weren't geeks. Macintosh expanded the market for personal computers to many more people.
- Macintosh was a rich programming environment with many technical capabilities—thus, it was a richer palette for software artists than Apple II and MS-DOS computers. This enabled programmers to create the software they had always wanted to.
- IBM dominated the application-software business for the IBM personal computer. Competing with IBM in that space was difficult because of the breadth of its distribution and the size of its salesforce. By contrast, Apple published far less software for Macintosh, so the Macintosh software market was a more level playing field.

Boich and I figured out that marketers liked expanding the penetration of computers, programmers liked the rich technology, and numbers-oriented people wanted to avoid overdependence on IBM. One of these stories usually resonated much more than the other two—based on whether the company was marketing driven, engineering driven, or finance driven.

Evangelism Wisdom

As evangelists, Boich and I used fervor and zeal to convince developers to create products for a computer with no installed base, minimal documentation, limited tools, and zero brand awareness. Maybe it was because we didn't know what we didn't know, but we succeeded. And along the way, this is what I learned about evangelism:

- Touch gold. It's very hard to evangelize crap. It's much easier to evangelize great stuff. I learned that the starting point of evangelism, and 90 percent of the battle, is having a great product. So your first challenge as an evangelist is to find or create something great to evangelize.

- Position as a "cause." A product, no matter how great, is ultimately just a collection of parts or snippets of code. A "cause," by contrast, changes lives. It's not enough to make a great product—you also need to position it and explain it as a way to improve lives. Steve Jobs didn't position an iPhone as $188 worth of components manufactured in China. Evangelists take the high ground and transcend the exchange of money for goods and services.

Localize the pitch. Don't describe your product using lofty, flowery terms like "revolutionary," "paradigm-shifting," and "curve-jumping." Macintosh wasn't "the third paradigm in personal computing." It simply (and powerfully) increased the productivity and creativity of one person with one computer. People don't buy "revolutions." They buy "aspirin" to fix the pain or "vitamins" to supplement their lives, so localize the pitch and keep it simple.

Look for agnostics; ignore people who belong to another religion. My experience was that the hardest person to convert to Macintosh was someone who worshiped MS-DOS. The easiest person was someone who had never used a personal computer before. If a person doesn't "get" your product or service after fifteen minutes, consider cutting your losses and moving on.

Let people test-drive the cause. Evangelists believe their potential customers are smart. Therefore, they don't bludgeon them with ads and promotions. Instead they provide ways for people to test-drive their products and then decide for themselves. Evangelists believe that their products are good—so good that they're not afraid of enabling people to try before they buy.

Learn to give a demo. "Evangelists who cannot give a great demo" is an oxymoron. If you can't give a great demo of your product, you cannot effectively evangelize it. Demoing should be second nature, maybe even reflexive. This is what made Steve Jobs the world's greatest evangelist for Apple's products.

Let people tell you how to evangelize them. We gave companies three different reasons to write Mac software. If they were amenable to supporting Macintosh, they usually told us which reason was the most appealing. Then we dropped the other two and concentrated on that one.

Provide a safe, easy first step. Remove all the barriers to the path of adopting your cause. Examples: (1) Revamping an entire IT infrastructure isn't necessary to try a new computer; (2) chaining yourself to a tree isn't necessary to join an environmental group; and (3) speaking a foreign language and owning a special keyboard aren't necessary to register for a website.

Ignore titles and pedigrees. Elitism is the enemy of evangelism. If you want to succeed as an evangelist, ignore people's backgrounds, accept people as they are, and treat everyone with respect and kindness. My experience is that a secretary, administrative aide, intern, part-timer, or trainee is more likely to embrace new products and services than a CXO or vice president.

Never lie. Lying is morally and ethically wrong. It also takes more energy because when you lie, it's necessary to keep track of what you said. If you always tell the truth, then there's nothing to keep track of. Evangelists evangelize great stuff, so they don't have to lie about features and benefits, and evangelists know their stuff, so they never have to lie to cover their ignorance.

👇 Remember your friends. Be nice to people on the way up, because you'll see them again on the way down. One of the most likely people to buy a Mac was an Apple II owner. One of the most likely people to buy an iPod was a Mac owner. One of the most likely people to buy whatever Apple puts out next is an iPhone owner.

Maybe it was because we didn't know what we didn't know, but we succeeded.

Writing

I wrote my first book, *The Macintosh Way*, in 1987. It explained how to do the right things the right way—essentially, what I learned when working in the Macintosh Division from 1983 to 1987.

When I wrote the book, I was the CEO of ACIUS, the software company I started after leaving Apple. My wife and I were living in an apartment on Hamilton Street in downtown Palo Alto. The place was small, so my work area was a closet no bigger than a telephone booth—maybe three feet by three feet.

I wrote the book using a Mac Plus. This model of Mac had 1 megabyte of RAM, an 800K floppy drive, and a 9-inch (23-centimeter) monochrome screen. So much for the romantic notion of writing with a gold-nib fountain pen in a room overlooking the Pacific Ocean.

Scott Foresman, a textbook company based in Illinois, published the book. However, *The Macintosh Way* wasn't a textbook, and I was a first-time author, so I was a risky bet for them. Were it not for my visibility in the Mac community, Scott Foresman would not have published the book.

Writing *The Macintosh Way* was easy, because I had accumulated so much stuff to say over the first thirty-three years of my life. When I finished the book, I thought I would never write another one because I had nothing more to say. It turns out that wasn't true, because *Wise Guy* is my fifteenth book.

> When I finished the book, I thought I would never write another one because I had nothing more to say.

1. *The Macintosh Way* (1987)
2. *Database 101* (1991)
3. *Selling the Dream* (1992)
4. *The Computer Curmudgeon* (1993)
5. *Hindsights* (1994)
6. *How to Drive Your Competition Crazy* (1995)
7. *Rules for Revolutionaries* (2000)
8. *The Art of the Start* (2004)
9. *Reality Check* (2011)
10. *What the Plus!* (September 2012)
11. *Enchantment* (December 2012)
12. *APE: Author, Publisher, Entrepreneu*r (2013)
13. *The Art of Social Media* (2014)
14. *The Art of the Start 2.0* (2015)
15. *Wise Guy* (2019)

Left to right: Poor Dad, Rich Dad.

This could be my last book, but I've said that fourteen times before.

My writing career was the catalyst for many great stories. Here are three of my favorites.

First, at least once a month, people would come up to me and say something along the lines of "I read your book, and it changed my life. Thank you so much for writing it." When I asked them which book they read, half the time they would say *Rich Dad Poor Dad* instead of a book that I had actually written.

Robert Kiyosaki wrote *Rich Dad Poor Dad*. All Asians look alike, but for clarification, I'm "Poor Dad, Poor

> "Guy must be really powerful because he dresses like a bum."

Dad" compared to Kiyosaki. I've even been introduced as the author of *Rich Dad Poor Dad* at speaking events.

During the 2018 SXSW conference, I tried to get into the press room, but the room monitor didn't let me in because I didn't have the proper press credentials. As I walked away, he caught up to me and asked, "Are you Guy Kawasaki?" I said that I was and figured he'd apologize and let me in to the press room.

Instead he said, "I read *Rich Dad Poor Dad* and loved it." And he still wouldn't let me in to the press room. As I wrote earlier, don't flatter yourself!

Second, I met Tom Wolfe, the famous author and journalist, through Rich Karlgaard, the publisher of *Forbes*. Wolfe's works include *The Bonfire of the Vanities*, *The Right Stuff*, and *The Electric Kool-Aid Acid Test*. He was famous for his high style, characterized by a white suit, white tie, white hat, and two-tone shoes.

I was never known for my high style. When I met him, I was in Silicon Valley business attire: jeans and a T-shirt. Karlgaard later told me that Wolfe said, "Guy must be really powerful because he dresses like a bum."

Third, the best onstage interview that I ever did was with Jane Goodall, the primatologist and anthropologist. The occasion was TEDx Palo Alto on September 12, 2018.

I had an offer to speak for another event, but I declined it. This cost me a few shekels, but I might never have gotten another chance to interview someone this cool. With hindsight, it was one of the best decisions of my career.

Goodall was awesome. There are people with great stories. There are people with great stage presence. There are few with both. She is one. These are my three favorite moments:

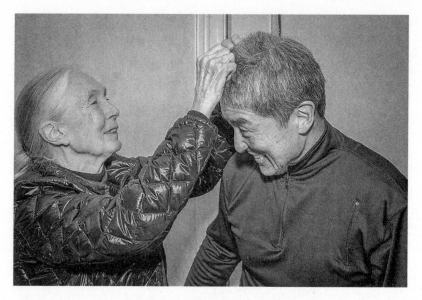

Jane Goodall grooming me like a chimpanzee.

- At the start of the interview, she transformed my introduction, "Me Guy, you Jane" (which I thought was very funny), to talk about the influence of Tarzan on her childhood. It was a very smooth transition.
- I asked her if chimpanzees were more intelligent than American politicians. Her response was that it depends on which American politicians I was referring to. Truer words were never spoken.
- She described an "alpha" chimpanzee that was all bluster and noise that tried to bully the others. I asked her if his term only lasted four years. Her response was that such leaders hopefully last only two years. (The event was two months before the 2018 midterm elections.)

Finally, look at the picture of her impersonating a chimpanzee grooming me. Many people told me that I was a good sport to endure this. They got it wrong. I asked her to do this in order to yield a more interesting picture than the usual shoulder-to-shoulder, "I'm hanging with a celebrity" shot. She was the good sport, not me.

Writing Wisdom

Fifteen books, hundreds of blog posts, dozens of articles, and thousands of social media posts have taught me many lessons about writing:

- Read to write. Great writers are great readers. The writing of others can inspire, motivate, and challenge you. In particular, you should read *If You Want to Write* by Brenda Ueland. As I mentioned before, that book changed my life.

- Have something to say. The only time you should write a book is when you have something important to convey. Fame, fortune, credibility, and other fantasies are not good reasons to do so. You should feel a moral obligation to write for the benefit of mankind. That's the test for whether the "book in you" should come out.

- Embrace the editing process. The key to writing is editing—that is, the willingness to refine your work through dozens of drafts after you think you are "done." No author spits out a good draft that only requires light editing.

☞ Buy a copy of *The Chicago Manual of Style*. Use it to answer your questions about grammar and punctuation. If nothing else, a copy of it on your desk will impress people who are knowledgeable about writing.

☞ Use Microsoft Word and create a "style" for every major component of your book. Each style is a set of formatting instructions such as font, size, justification, and spacing. Styles make it easy to reorganize your book using Word's outline view and easy to convert your document to a page-composition program such as Adobe InDesign. At a minimum, I suggest these styles:

– Heading 1 or Chapter
– Heading 2 or Section
– Heading 3 or Subheading
– First paragraph
– Normal paragraph

The only time you should write a book is when you have something important to convey.

☞ Search for every instance of "ly" to hunt down and kill adverbs, and search for every instance of "be" to hunt down and kill the passive voice. Note: make sure there's a space after "ly" and "be" when you search for them so you don't find "ly" or "be" within words.

☞ Go on a "which" hunt by searching for every instance of "which" and "that" to ensure you're using the right word for the context.

☞ Make a thumbnail of the cover of your book and look at it next to the thumbnails on an Amazon page. Can you even read the title?

☞ Spend two hours building up your social media following for every hour you spend writing. Start this the day you decide to write a book, because you'll find that marketing a book is harder than writing it.

☞ Search for double spaces and replace them with a single space as the last step.

Public Speaking

For many people, public speaking is one of the most stressful activities. This isn't true for me. Since 1987 I have given more than fifty speeches a year to audiences of as many as 25,000 people. Speaking in front of groups has become second nature—in fact, it takes a thousand-person audience to get me psyched up these days.

My speaking career began in 1987, when I published *The Macintosh Way*. A Macintosh software company—I can't remember which one—asked me to speak to its employees about the book. I told them my fee was $2,500, and they agreed. When I started speaking to large audiences, though, I was far from comfortable. This was because I had seen Steve Jobs in action, and measuring up to him was an intimidating task. Luckily, the odds that you work for someone who's as good a speaker as Steve Jobs are zero.

I've had many interesting experiences as the result of my speaking career. Here are three of the best:

First, one sequence of the James Bond movie *Skyfall* featured a

On the roof of the Grand Bazaar. Think: GuyFall.

motorcycle chase on the roof of the Grand Bazaar in Istanbul, Turkey. Shortly after the film opened, I gave a keynote speech for Turkcell, the leading mobile service provider there. I asked if I could go on the roof where the scene was shot. To my amazement, Turkcell made this happen.

Second, Pat O'Neill, the CEO of O'Neill, the surfing equipment and attire company in Santa Cruz, asked me to speak to his sales team. There was no monetary compensation. Instead, I received the IP address and password for a video camera on the roof of O'Neill's father's home on East Cliff Drive in Santa Cruz. This is one of the most exclusive surfing cameras in the world and has provided me with one of the best views of surfing conditions there.

Third, the organizers of a tech conference in Russia wanted me to speak at their event, but the appearance would have conflicted with some family activities. The organizers wanted me so badly that they not only paid my fees but also flew my buddy Will Mayall and me to and from Russia via a combination of Lufthansa first-class seats and a private jet. I was in Russia for a total of twelve hours. The whole trip took thirty-six hours.

Public Speaking Wisdom

One morning in the fall of 2015, I met with an African American entrepreneur who told me that he had already given a company presentation that day and had one more in the afternoon. He asked me if I had any tips to make his presentation better.

In turn, I asked him, "Is your background black?" And he responded, "Yeah, I'm from a multicultural family from Atlanta." I had a good laugh, then told him, "I can see that you're black. I'm asking if the background of your *PowerPoint* slides is black."

> "Is your background black?"

My theory is that white text on a black background is easier to read than black text on a white background. Also, black text on a white background says, "I created a new document and started typing."

White text on a black background shows that you're a PowerPoint ninja master who knows how to create a master page and change the color of text.

In addition to using a black background, this is what I learned about speaking:

☞ Ask for a small room. It's easier to entertain and inform an audience that's packed into a room, so try to get the smallest venue that you can. It's a mental game. You will think,

People are so interested in my presentation that it's standing-room only. The audience will think, *He's such a good speaker that there's standing-room only.*

🤙 Befriend the audio-visual team. Don't treat the people in the back of the room and behind the screen as if they are your minions. You want them to want you to succeed, because they can ruin your presentation, if not your career.

🤙 Pre-circulate. Before you speak, don't hide in the green room or backstage. Get out and circulate with the audience—especially the people in the front rows. When you are onstage, you want to look out and see familiar, friendly faces. You need the positive energy of those people who want you to succeed.

🤙 Customize your beginning. Use LinkedIn to find connections to the people in your audience—schools, companies, interests—whatever it takes. Use this information to break the ice. If you're talking to a company whose products you use, mention that—or better yet, take a picture of yourself with the product. You can also show a picture of yourself traveling in the country where you're speaking.

🤙 Take off like an F/A-18 Hornet fighter jet, not an Airbus A380. The fighter jets that take off from an aircraft carrier get into the air from a runway that's approximately one thousand feet long. An Airbus A380 needs

I used this picture to start a speech in Russia: "I had no idea you Russians had such big balls." And this was in 2008, before the Russians made Donald Trump the president of the United States.

approximately two miles. Good speeches take off like a fighter jet and don't rumble along for two miles before making it into the air.

Use a maximum of ten slides, if you use slides at all. You'll be lucky to get ten points across in a presentation. Less is more. There's a reason David

> You'll be lucky to get ten points across in a presentation.

Letterman didn't use a top twenty-five or top fifty list: no audience can handle more than ten key points.

👆 Make the type size on your slides bigger. I suggest at least 30 points. FYI: Steve Jobs used 190-point text. The bigger the text, the fewer words fit on a page, and the more you'll communicate. Keep cutting words until your text fits your slides. Less is more.

👆 Limit your presentation to twenty minutes. This is because meetings often start late and end early, and you may not be able to make your Windows laptop work with the projector in a timely manner. TED Talks are only eighteen minutes. It's better to end early and have time for questions and answers than to end late and not cover your key points.

👆 Tell stories. Always tell stories. Use them to illustrate your key points. Stories are ten times more powerful than bullshit adjectives such as "revolutionary," "innovative," and "cool." I believe in stories so much that this book is a collection of stories.

If you do these simple things, your presentations will be better than 95 percent of those of other speakers.

One more wisdom that I gained from speaking: people throughout the world are more similar than they are different. Maybe it's because I interact with the same kind of audiences—tech, entrepreneurial, marketing—but the people I've met consistently want to support their families, create cool products, and raise happy and productive kids.

In other words, tribalism is overrated and for losers.

Social Media

The first time I looked at Twitter, I thought it was dumb. My initial exposure, like many people's, was the Twitter home page, where I saw dozens of "Lonelyboy15s" tweeting that his dog rolled over and "TiffanyfromLAs" tweeting that the line at Starbucks was long.

My aha moment with Twitter, and with social media in general, occurred when I searched for my own name, the companies I was associated with, and the companies I competed against. It became clear that social media was a great way to promote products, provide information and support, and monitor the competition.

My attitude toward social media is pragmatic: it is a means to an end. The "end" is the successful promotion of the products, companies, and causes. My goal was not "social" in the sense of making new friends. By 2018, I had figured out I could handle no more than fifteen relationships in a meaningful way.

That said, my efforts weren't about manipulation but, rather, to earn attention. My social media posts provide information, assistance, and entertainment—and in exchange I want to earn the privilege of running my "pledge drives," which are promotions for my companies, books, and speeches. This is the Wikipedia/NPR Donation Test that I mentioned earlier.

> My attitude toward social media is pragmatic: it is a means to an end. The "end" is the successful promotion of the products, companies, and causes.

Social Media Wisdom

In 2018, I had approximately twelve million followers across LinkedIn, Twitter, Facebook, Google+, and Instagram—and I did not buy any of them. I was considered one of the most influential social media users in the world.

I was skeptical about how much real clout "influencers" have, but being an influencer has bestowed three benefits:

- A presumption of credibility. Though simplistic and unjustified, the prevalent thinking is that people with more followers are opinion leaders who influence the behavior of others. My being considered an influencer, in turn, has led to speaking, endorsement, and consulting opportunities.
- Astounding customer service. For example, whenever I have had any issues with Comcast, three or four trucks would show up to take care of my problem in less than twenty-four hours. I could tweet about any brand and immediately receive support, because brands are so afraid of negative feedback on social media.
- A flow of freebies, such as cameras, tech accessories, watches, surfboards, clothing, food, and tickets for events. This is a "1%" problem, but I started turning freebies down, because giving them to me was a waste of time and money for the companies.

This list of the benefits of being an "influencer" is more humble-bragging than educational, but here's the wisdom I'd like to pass on to you about social media:

🤙 Add value to people's lives. Remember NPR's model of providing great content to earn the right to solicit donations and run pledge drives that raise $90 million? Provide value, and social media becomes a fast, free, ubiquitous, and powerful tool.

🤙 Think Tinder, not eHarmony. People make instant decisions about whether you are worth paying attention to on social media. If social media were online dating, it would be Tinder (swipe right or swipe left), not eHarmony (twenty-nine dimensions of compatibility).

🤙 Optimize your avatar and cover page. The first data that people use to make their instant decision are your avatar and cover page. Your avatar should project you as a likable, trustworthy, and competent person. It should contain only your face—no other people, plants, animals, or objects. Your cover photo should establish that you are an interesting person, so tell your story with it.

> Transparency is overrated if you're an asshole.

🤙 Be positive or be silent. Transparency is overrated if you're an asshole. If you don't have something positive to say, shut up and keep scrolling. I don't advise making it obvious that you're a jerk. The audience you care about is everyone who reads the comments not the person you're fighting with.

Repeat your posts. I once tweeted the same thing three times in a five-minute span and noticed that there were no complaints and that each tweet was equally effective. This led me to intentionally repeat my tweets. Some people may object, but you'll achieve far more views if you learn to ignore the small number of grumbles and repeat your posts.

Keep experimenting. Don't assume that what the experts recommend is optimal or true—me included. The only thing that won't change is the value of experimentation.

11

Ohana

What people in the world think of you
is really none of your business.

—Martha Graham

In case you didn't know, *ohana* is the Hawaiian word for "family." It is not limited to blood or marriage but can include anyone with whom you have a deep relationship. I asked members of my *ohana* to write about the wisdom they acquired through an interaction with me. Here are their stories.

Craig Stein, surfing buddy

Craig Stein lives in San Diego, California. He is the founder of The Hired Executive, an eight-week program for executives who are in careers. Most important, Stein is one of my surfing buddies.

My introduction to Guy was in 2005. I was an MBA student, and Guy was giving a presentation at Ohio State University. At the end of his speech, Guy recounted a story about his speaking fees.

When you are an A-list speaker such as Guy, you command a hefty sum for your speeches. While some organizations take the news in stride, others resist and try to negotiate, if not lowball.

Guy shared what his next move would be if the second scenario played out. When the client hesitated, he would put the following counteroffer on the table:

"Hire me to give the speech. If I don't get a standing ovation, I will waive my fees entirely. However, if I do receive a standing ovation, you pay me twice the fee."

A betting man. A confident man. A man with chutzpah. A funny man, too!

An icon in the world of entrepreneurship had demonstrated what might appear to be a Wild West mentality. But that's not what was going on. Guy taught me that if you played your cards right, you could be dancing all the way to the bank. The capitalist in me was wowed.

And no, no one has ever taken him up on the offer.

Wisdom

Commit to excellence. Who wouldn't want to receive double their market rate? But Guy's lesson was so much richer than that. In essence, he was demonstrating the value that exists in being good at what you do.

People will always seek out and handsomely compensate those who have reached the top of their field. Negotiating a double-or-nothing deal is not the objective. The commitment to your path of excellence is what counts.

Once that level of excellence is reached, exercising the attained physical prowess is no longer the focus. Rather, prowess provides a deep, quiet confidence that surfaces in tough negotiations, casual conversations, and even within your private thoughts as it would for a martial arts sensei.

Bruna Martinuzzi, Macintosh user

Bruna Martinuzzi is the author of *The Leader as a Mensch: Become the Kind of Person Others Want to Follow* and a presentation coach based in Vancouver, Canada.

It was around 9:00 p.m. one evening a little over a decade ago that I experienced yet another frustration with my old laptop and decided that I would buy a state-of-the-art new one the very next day. I did some online searching and couldn't decide which laptop to choose.

I had come across Guy Kawasaki's humorous saying in his now famous video clip about the 10, 20, 30 PowerPoint

Rule: "You're using a Windows laptop. It will take you 45 min-
utes to make it work with the projector." I thought, Why not
ask him?

So I did a search for his name and found an email address.
In an impulse move, I emailed him right then and there, briefly
introduced myself, and asked him if he could help me with ad-
vice on which laptop to buy.

To my amazement, I received a response within ten minutes!
I couldn't believe it. Of course, he recommended a Mac! This
was in addition to ensuring that I bought a solid-state drive and
Apple Care. I thought, What a kind man, so generous with his
advice, just like that!

This might seem like a story about "ask, and you shall re-
ceive." It's about that, for sure. But it's also about something
else. I was pleasantly surprised and grateful that someone of
his stature would take the time to answer a stranger up north
who might be of no use to him. I wasn't buying anything, I wasn't
offering anything. Just a missile from cyberspace to someone with
a crowded inbox. His kindness made an impression on me.

Wisdom

Help people who cannot help you. A measure of a person's goodness
is how they treat someone who can be of no use to them. Guy
showed this by his action that evening. After this experience, I al-
ways remember Guy's action when I am reluctant to respond to
people I don't know. His example has been an inspiration to me to
this day.

Nic Kawasaki, son

Nic Kawasaki is my oldest son. He wrote this at the age of twenty-four.

One night in December 2017, I was back at my childhood home in Atherton. It was around ten at night, and I was getting ready to leave for an adult hockey league game in Redwood City.

Because it was late, below forty degrees out, and most of the lights in the house had been turned off, I assumed that my family would all be asleep as I stealthily packed my hockey bag and threw it into the trunk of my car.

But right when I began to pull out of the driveway, I noticed a light on in the back of our family's minivan. I rolled over to investigate from behind the wheel of the electric car I was driving at the time and saw a figure hunched over in the driver's seat of the minivan. I was a little nervous by this point, but as I leaned over and turned a light on, I saw that it was just my dad, bent over reading something.

I asked him what he was doing, and he said he was putting something away in the car. Classic Guy Kawasaki move. I took this as one of my dad's moments where he was trying to do something small that could really wait until the morning, but that he had to do it right then and there, just as his father would have before him (something that my mom always teases him about).

We spoke for a few moments, and as I was getting ready to tell him good night and peel off into the dark Atherton night, my dad asked me where I was going. I told him I had a game down at the Redwood City rink, and with a look of concern and a glance down at his watch, he asked me what time.

I replied that we had the late game slot at 10:30 p.m., and he said that he might come watch. I thanked him and told him he didn't have to see his washed-up son play, sort of shrugging off his comment as I drove down the driveway and toward the rink.

As I was taking part in the pregame warm-up, I skated around the ice, getting the blood flowing and the wrists warmed up by firing pucks into the empty net, when one of my teammates came up to me and gave a nod to the front of the lower seating area of the ice rink.

"Did Guy come to watch us play?"

At first I didn't see anything, so I gave the guy a shove and said, "Yeah, right." But then he repeated the question and pointed again, this time with a more urgent look in his eye. So to humor him, I looked over and squinted. Holy shit, there he was. My dad, sitting there all alone in his jeans and sweatshirt, watching me play a meaningless adult hockey league game in the middle of the night. Honestly, my first thought was, Oh, man, Mom is going to be pissed if he's tired and groggy tomorrow.

The first period began, and I scored a couple of goals, and it felt good to show the old man that I could still skate despite being a corporate sellout. At that point I was just happy to put some pucks in the net while he was still there, and I assumed he would leave after about the first half hour or so. But then the second period ended, and he was still there.

After a bit, the buzzer rang, signifying the end of the game, and I still saw him sitting in the stands. I couldn't help but be brought back to when he would come to every game I played when I was younger and in college.

He went home after the game ended, and after drying my gear I walked into the kitchen and saw him. He complimented my game and offered a few words of encouragement as I grabbed some food and prepared to go to sleep. It was something along the lines of "You sure can still score some goals." I smiled and said thanks, wished him a good night, and then hit the hay. But I would never forget that night.

When my dad asked me if I would like to write a chapter, I said sure. I love my dad, and he has imparted an incredible amount of wisdom, either intentionally or unintentionally, to me throughout the years up until my life now as a working adult.

However, I had no idea what I was going to write about until that night. That experience got me thinking about how my dad has been as a father and a man. It was that night that inspired my hindsight.

Despite my dad's jam-packed travel schedule, he always made an effort to stay involved in his kids' lives, something that I don't imagine was easy. Hell, I have trouble just coming to work every day from nine to five. Multiply that times four kids and a travel schedule that never seems to end, and I get stressed out just thinking about it.

I played a lot of sports in high school. There were literally hundreds of football games and lacrosse games, and countless road trips for my ice hockey teams. My dad was always there. He once chartered a private jet so that he could speak in Detroit and still make my high school "senior" football game.

He would even drive up to Oakland on a Friday night, crawl through Bay Area traffic, just so that he could see me play club hockey while I was at Cal. I will always remember the sight of him sitting there in the freezing rink, one of probably about five people on most nights, cheering us on while shooting photos of the team playing through a comically giant camera lens.

And we haven't even touched on his illustrious playing career. He started playing hockey when Noah and I took it up over ten years ago, and only recently stopped playing frequently. This is because of his newfound love of surfing, the sport that my younger siblings took up. I remember when I was a little kid, I would just come watch him play on Saturday nights and get to hang out with him and the team in the locker room afterward.

We played hockey together countless times, usually on the same team, although I did like to school him when he had the wrong-colored jersey. To be honest, there were many times that I was annoyed at my dad for a lousy pass, missed shot, or turnover, but I was always grateful that he was there and that he really took an interest in my life. Now he has been doing the same with surfing for my younger siblings.

Now, I know what you may be thinking: fathers are always there for their kids when they are growing up. I agree. But I wasn't a kid that night at the rink in Redwood City. At least in my mind I wasn't anymore. I was twenty-four, I had a full-time job, and I lived in an apartment in San Francisco.

But my dad still came and watched me, even though I was a bird that had left the proverbial nest. I could see the joy in his *face and feel the warmth in his voice as we chatted after the game that night while standing in our kitchen. It made me realize that even though I am technically now an adult, I will always be his son, and he will always be there for me.*

Wisdom

Put your family before anything else. As my father has done for me and our family, I will be there for mine no matter how busy I may become, or what other obligations I may have as I get older. I also realized that no matter how old I get, when I get married or (gulp) have children, I will always be my father's son, and he will always love me like one.

Peg Fitzpatrick, coauthor

Peg Fitzpatrick and I coauthored *The Art of Social Media*. We met in December 2012 when she asked me to appear in her Twitter book club. She is also the person who told me to help Canva back in 2014.

On a visit to Silicon Valley, I ran an errand with Guy to pick up photos at Walgreens. We went into the store, and Guy picked up his photos and then grabbed a gallon of milk, bread, peanut butter, and jelly.

After paying we left the store, and Guy walked over to a homeless man who was sitting off to the side of the entrance. I didn't notice him on the way in. Guy gave him all the groceries

that he had purchased. He didn't make a big deal of it, and
naturally the man was appreciative.

It was such a thoughtful act. Few people would think of, or
take the time to do, something like this. People might not expect
a selfless act from a famous speaker and author, but it's exactly
the type of person that Guy is. I'd be willing to guess he doesn't
even remember doing this.

Wisdom

Help when you can, where you can. Instead of looking at the bigger
picture of homelessness and not being able to solve the problem, Guy
zoomed in to assist one person. It didn't take much time or much
money.

It took only one person seeing another person on the street and
helping. Imagine if we all did one selfless act like this a day. We
need more people to think like this in our world.

By the way, Peg is right. I don't remember buying food for the
homeless person.

Shawn Welch, coauthor

Shawn Welch lives in Kansas City and works as an iOS engineer for
Square, Inc., on the Cash App. He has written two books on iPhone
development, and we coauthored the *Wall Street Journal* best seller
APE: Author, Publisher, Entrepreneur.

We first met in February 2012 when Guy was writing What the Plus! *and needed help converting bullet points from Microsoft Word to the Kindle Direct Publishing (KDP) platform. I responded to his public plea for help (on Google+) and sent an email offering my assistance.*

To my surprise, Guy sent me his entire manuscript almost immediately and outlined the problems he was having. He had no idea who I was or what my background was. He only knew I said I could help.

Shawn's sample bullet points on a Kindle.

That evening I converted a chapter and sent it back to him along with a picture of his book on my Kindle. If you haven't learned it by now, Guy is very much a show, don't tell person. Show the magic first, then explain what you did.

I'm not sure what I expected, but it certainly wasn't what happened. After some back and forth over the next couple days, Guy asked me to lay out and produce What the Plus! *and for the next four months we worked side by side launching that book. Then that summer we were having coffee in Palo Alto and decided others would benefit from what we had learned together, so we decided to coauthor* APE: Author, Publisher, Entrepreneur.

How I met Guy is not unique; it's a pattern with how Guy finds and works with new people. In a previous chapter, Guy mentioned his "Golden Touch"—not that whatever he touches turns to gold but whatever is gold, he touches.

He used that in the context of a great product, but he extends that philosophy to great people as well. I've seen Guy hire unproven copywriters, cover designers, social media consultants, and more. Guy looks for competence, not a résumé. He isn't afraid to admit what he doesn't know and surrounds himself with people who not only fill in the gaps, but who also have their own spark to bring to the table.

Wisdom

🤙 *Admit when you don't know something and don't be afraid to seek out help. Don't think that you're above learning from someone else.*

🤙 *Look for competence, not a résumé. Don't be afraid to give unproven people a chance.*

Bonus Story

When Guy originally asked me to contribute to this book I was honored. I consider him a true friend and wrote what I felt was an honest depiction of the story you just read. He cut more than half of it. And the parts he cut were the nice things I said about him.

Guy might fly first class and share stories of nice cars and big trips. But when it comes to the way he carries himself as a person, he is the first to decline a compliment. He is humble in his abilities and quick to give credit to others.

I'm adding this back in on my second edit (let's see if he cuts it a second time) because I think there's some important wisdom there as well.

Wisdom

Be humble, be relational. Nobody gets where they are without the help of others in one way or another. Be quick to reward those who helped you along the way. Focus on amicable relationships and genuinely work to help others succeed without the thought of a quid pro quo.

Noah Kawasaki, son

Noah Kawasaki is my second oldest son. He wrote this at the age of twenty-three.

In 2017, our family bought a house in Santa Cruz. Almost immediately, my dad started meeting everyone and making connections left and right. Also, I was in the beginning of my junior year at UCLA and was starting to think more seriously about a future career path. What industry? What company? What department? I wasn't very sure.

My dad's enthusiasm for this new place had him fantasizing about me finding a great internship nearby and spending the summer living, working, and surfing in Santa Cruz. He said I would be "living the dream."

So sometime later I got a text from my dad saying that he'd found three cool companies: O'Neill, Inboard, and Looker. I already knew what O'Neill was. Inboard was a new electric skateboard company, which I also thought was pretty cool.

Then there was this company called Looker. It seemed like this super cool, fun, and challenging new tech company in Santa Cruz. I spent a lot of time researching them on Google, watching their YouTube videos, checking out ratings on Glassdoor, etc. The more time I spent reading about Looker, the more I knew that Looker was the one.

My dad texted me again a couple days later and told me to rank these three companies in the order I would like to work for them. I replied with my listing, though the one that really mattered was Looker. He replied saying, "Hardest order . . . ," as in Looker would be the hardest one to pull off.

Fast-forward a couple of months, and I had been exchanging emails with one of Looker's recruiters, having phone calls with the director of the customer support team, and having lunch in the office with my would-be managers. I don't know what the exact actions my dad took to make this happen, but it was definitely swaying Looker to consider my résumé.

I ended up accepting an internship offer and "living the dream" that summer in Santa Cruz. It was such an incredible experience of working, learning, making friends, being stressed out, and having fun that I accepted a full-time return offer before going back down to UCLA for senior year.

Because of my dad, I was able to have a worry-free senior year, got a job at a great company straight out of school, and still get to see my family every week.

Wisdom

Give your children infinite opportunities and every advantage to be successful. Support them when they want to try learning something new. Don't be afraid to ask others for favors.

Bonus Wisdom

Help your children find great jobs nearby and give them indefinite free rent if you want them to live close to you.

Nate Kawasaki, son

Nate is my youngest son. He wrote this at the age of thirteen.

One day my dad picked me up from school, and out of the blue I asked him if we could get some dry ice. I was really surprised that he said yes. When we picked up dry ice, the guy who helped us told us not to close the car windows because we could lose oxygen and suffocate.

First thing I said when we got home was, "Let's open the pool and put the dry ice in the hot tub." I also got our GoPro so we could see what it looked like underwater. When we put the dry ice *in, my dad and I had a blast. It felt like we were coming out of a movie scene with smoke in the background.*

Then for some reason (as my dad mentioned earlier in this book), my brain thought we should put dry ice in a plastic bottle and then put water in it. So we got a plastic bottle, put dry ice in it, filled it up with water really quick, tightened the cap, and threw it in the water. One Mississippi, two Mississippi, and then POP!

It was a sound like a gunshot. My dad and I looked at each other and thought, Like, what did we just do? *Come to find out, it was very dangerous.*

Wisdom

Google the safety of things before you try them.

Nohemi Kawasaki, daughter

Nohemi is my daughter. She wrote this at the age of sixteen.

Most times when we go surfing, my dad talks to at least one new person in the water. Although he is initially being polite and getting to know them, next thing you know, he ends up letting his new acquaintance try his board. If they keep talking, within an hour or two, my dad will invite his new friend up to the house.

Usually, my father opens the garage and shows him or her the abundance of surfboards that we have and asks if they would like to try any of them next time. I cannot even keep track of the number of people who have come through and used our outdoor shower, hose, surfboards, and wetsuits.

Through my dad's giving spirit, he has created a network of relationships in all sorts of different areas. My dad has shown me that it is very important to create and maintain strong relationships. If you do, you will always be able to go to a person if you, or someone else you know, is in need.

Because of this, I have learned to be kind and giving to people, even people I do not know. Everyone should do at least one thing generous every day because it makes those around you happy, and it even makes you feel happy when you do something good for someone else.

Dad, you may not realize the impact you have made on my life, but the idea of being generous toward anyone, even people you don't know, has led me to become a better person. I know I may not always be the sweetest girl, especially to you, but I will always try to be generous just like you.

Wisdom

Be generous. My father has taught me numerous things, such as how to ride a bike, how to write, how to be responsible—I wish I could say surf, but that is not the case.

Rick Kot, editor

Rick Kot is my editor at Penguin. As you'll read, we've been working together for twenty-eight mind-boggling years.

I first encountered Guy in 1989 during a lunchtime stroll through the McGraw-Hill bookstore in Manhattan. While browsing that day I noticed I'd just missed by a few minutes a signing by the author of The Macintosh Way.

I'd only recently bought my first Macintosh and was completely under its spell, so that title was pretty much catnip for me, and I left the store with a (signed) copy of the book in hand. Guy's evangelism was so engaging and infectious that I recommended to a colleague that he acquire paperback rights to the book, which HarperCollins published the following year.

I later wound up taking on editorial responsibility for The Macintosh Way, *which began a partnership and friendship that has lasted—can it be true?—twenty-eight years.* Wise Guy *is our eighth book together, and for all the years I've known Guy, I realized I didn't really know him until I read this manuscript.*

Our relationship has involved a lot of fraternal chopsbusting, and I've grown so accustomed to being steamrolled, corrected, arm-twisted, argued with, snookered, and generally instructed in how the world really works by him that I was unprepared to find in these pages The Other Guy—this thoughtful, heartfelt, and, yes, sweet-natured man whose enthusiasm for his various jobs is outshone only by his love for his hobbies and, especially, his family.

Wikipedia says that the concept of ohana *"emphasizes that families are bound together and members must cooperate and remember one another." Working as an editor with a writer is by necessity a cooperative effort, one that involves a great deal of trust on both sides, as bringing a book into the world is no easy process.*

I often think that part of my responsibility involves saving an author from himself, but Guy's shown me often enough that I need to be saved from myself, as well (even if I'm never going to come around to agreeing with him on his disparagement of the passive voice).

Our karmic balance sheet at this point is probably just about even: When I suggested he write Art of the Start, *he asked, "Who needs another start-up book?"; when he fought for the cover of* Enchantment, *I asked, "Who's going to buy that?" Both books, in fact, were great successes, and at least one of us was humbled by the experience.*

Wisdom

Collaboration can be an infinitely rewarding (and entertaining) process when both parties bring not only their expertise to the table but also the willingness to put up a good fight, a sense of humor, and ultimately the flexibility to know when to capitulate. Collaborations built over the course of many years are the most gratifying of all.

(May I point out that the other Wisdom sections start with a verb? Rick's starts with "collaboration," a noun and the hideous passive voice.)

Nic Kawasaki. And while we're at it, here are the rest of the kids.

Noah Kawasaki.

Nohemi Kawasaki.

Nate Kawasaki.

Postpartum

Scared is what you're feeling. Brave is what you're doing.

—Emma Donoghue

Thank you for reading my book. Living these stories helped me; I hope reading them helped you. I want to leave you with a list of my top ten wisdoms.

 1. *Get high and to the right.* The key to career success is to acquire unique skills that are valuable. Unique skills that aren't valuable don't matter. Valuable skills that aren't unique don't set you apart. Life is good when you

Unique

X

Valuable

High and to the right, FTW!

are unique and valuable, so be the best at something that's in demand.

2. *Adopt a growth mind-set.* Learning is a process, not an event. It doesn't end when you complete your formal education. If you've "got it made," risk your self-image and pride by trying something you're not good at. No matter how much you know, you can still learn more. The more you learn, the more you learn (and earn).

3. *Embrace grit.* The flip side of adopting a growth mind-set is embracing hard work and determination—in other words, grit. Achieving success is hard work. Great ideas are easy, but implementation is hard. Intelligence and talent without grit is inconsequential.

4. *Smile.* The more you smile and laugh, the more you will smile and laugh. The more you smile and laugh, the easier life gets. You can never go wrong being nice, and there's no such thing as being too nice.

5. *Default to yes.* Assume that people are good and default to helping them. The upside of defaulting to yes far exceeds the downside of being used. This doesn't mean you'll never say no, but say no after you've collected information, not because no is your default.

6. *Raise the tide.* You don't need algebra, calculus, and geometry to succeed. You only need to understand that life is not a zero-sum game. Your loss is not someone else's gain. Someone else's loss is not your gain. A rising tide lifts all boats, so do what you can to fill the ocean, lake, pond, pool, or bathtub.

7. *Pay it forward.* There is a karmic scoreboard in the sky. The net balance of this scoreboard determines your fate. Do good things, help people out, and make the world a better place. These actions are an investment in your future. Even if I'm wrong, why take a chance on something as important as fate?

8. *Examine everything.* Life isn't all unicorns and pixie dust. Examine everything and do not go through life on Level 5 completely autonomous driving, to use a car analogy. Unexamined driving can kill you—so can unexamined living. But don't get me wrong: I'm recommending skepticism, not negativity.

9. *Never lie, seldom shade.* This is the pragmatist's guide to honesty. Lying takes too much time and energy, because you have to keep track of how you lied. Instead, always tell the truth, and seldom shade the truth. The truth will set you free.

10. *Enable people to pay you back.* With the recommendation to default to yes and pay it forward, why enable

people to pay you back? The answer is that you honor people by enabling them to pay you back. It relieves them of feeling indebted, and their ability to reciprocate fosters their sense of self-worth.

Now go forth and dance to your own music. This isn't carte blanche, but two indisputable facts are that life is short and you can't make everyone happy. The logical conclusion is to dance to your own music before the music stops—as my son Noah says, "YOLO!" Now go live this way.

Guy Kawasaki

Recommended Reading

There is no greater recommendation than when an author tells you to read someone else's book.

—Guy Kawasaki

If You Want to Write by Brenda Ueland. This book empowered me to write. If you're experiencing doubt or resistance in any endeavor, not just writing, this is the book for you.

Drive: The Surprising Truth About What Motivates Us by Daniel Pink. A great explanation of why money and perks are not the only factors to recruiting and keeping great employees.

Mindset: The New Psychology of Success by Carol Dweck. I love how Dweck explains that your mind-set and outlook can change everything. This is the most powerful personal-psychology book that I've read.

Influence: The Psychology of Persuasion, Revised Edition, by Robert Cialdini. Written by the master himself, the foundation, IMHO, of all books about the science of persuasion and influence.

Absolute Value: What Really Influences Customers in the Age of (Nearly) Perfect Information by Itamar Simonson and Emanuel Rosen. When information is fast, free, and ubiquitous, all the rules must change.

Index

Google can bring you back 100,000 answers.
A librarian can bring you back the right one.

—Neil Gaiman

"The Ability to Live with Incongruence: Aintegration—The Concept and Its Operationalization" (Lomranz and Benyamini), 18
absolutes, 49
Absolute Value (Simonson and Rosen), 236
accidental innovation, 85–86
ACIUS, 64, 65, 101, 192
adjectives vs. stories, 87–88, 204
Adobe, 72, 96
Adobe InDesign, 198
adoption, 133–36
adverbs, avoiding, 14, 198

advice, sharing and accepting, 11
agreement, 71–73
Ahern, Mike, 155
"aintegration," 18
Akau, Trudy, 10–11, 15
Alaskan Air Command, 83
Aldus Corporation, 72
Amazon, 95, 168
ambiguity, 17–18
American Institute of Graphic Arts (AIGA), 81–82
America Online, 105
America's Got Talent, 82

ancestry of author, 1–8
anchoring, 61–62
animal welfare, 3
APE: Author, Publisher, Entrepreneur, 220
Apple
    and America Online, 105–6
    and app development policy, 170
    Apple II computers, 52–53, 91, 188, 192
    Apple stores, 162–64
    Apple University, 52, 184
    and author's career trajectory, 64–65,
        68–71, 77, 80, 101–2, 109, 184, 192
    and author's education, 11
    and author's wife, 131
    and Boich, 21–22, 27
    and denied promotions, 62–63
    and hiring of author, 51–57
    and intellectual property lawsuits, 60–62
    and Jobs's influence, 73–76
    key lessons from, 73–76, *74*
    mistakes and opportunities, 86–87
    and power of stories, 88
    and product enthusiasts, 66–68
    and product evangelism, 188,
        190–91, 212
    product positioning challenges,
        71–73, 91
    and taking initiative, 59–60
    and tech support work, 30
    and "thinking different," 181
    truthfulness in job settings, 57–58
Arrow, Pearson, 159
The Art of Social Media (Kawasaki and
    Fitzpatrick), 95, 217
The Art of the Start (Kawasaki), 227
Ashton-Tate, 62, 63, 64
Asian American culture, 39–40
Ask Group, 30
assembly languages, 111–12
audio-visual teams, 202
authority, respecting, 16–17
automobiles, 25–28, *27. See also*
    Mercedes-Benz.
avatars, 206
Azril, Ade Harnusa, 81–82

Banff Venture Forum, 107
Barnes, Susan, 59–60
Barry, Bob, 12
benefits of products, 90
Benioff, Marc, 112–13, *113*

Benyamini, Yael, 18
Berklee College of Music, 3
bluffing, 60–61
Bob Shapell School of Social Work, 18
Boesche, Robert, 20
Boich, Mike, *52*
    and author's career trajectory, 21–22,
        52–55, 101
    automobile enthusiasm, 22, 27–28
    and product evangelism, 188–89
Bonobos, 94, 95
boycotts, 81–82
Brainerd, Paul, 72
branding, 205–7
Branson, Richard, 113, *114*
Bratcher, Lucille, 12
brick-and-mortar stores, 95
Broughall, Steve, 83
Brown, Jack, 60–62
Brown and Bain, 60
Bush, George W., 36
business
    and accidental innovations, 85–87
    author's career trajectory, 101–3
    and customer gratification, 94–95
    and focus on providing benefits, 89–90
    and ignoring the inconsequential, 99–100
    and passion, 83–85
    and power of small changes, 92–93
    and power of stories, 87–88
    and salesmanship, 77–80
    and second followers, 90–92
    and startup companies, 95–99
    and unpaid opportunity, 81–83
bystander effect, 145–47

Canadians, 121–22
Canva, 77, 88, 95–98, 102, 217
career planning, 39–40, 51–57, 101–2,
    221–22, 231–32
Carrillo Dining Commons, 92
Case, Steve, 106–8
causes, 189
challenges, 15, 75
Chan, Jackie, 33, *34*
change, 7–8, 46, 171. *See also* quitting.
charity, 217–18
Cheeze, 102
The Chicago Manual of Style, 14, 198
China, 2
Cialdini, Robert, 236

Cinar, Baha, 102
Civil Rights Act (1964), 37
Clark, Jeff, 155–57
Clinton, Bill, 47–48, 115
Clinton, Hillary, *116,* 117
coaching
    impact on life trajectory, 11–12, 15, 150
    and parenting skills, 141
    and quitting, 42
    and surfing, 156, 161–62, 165
codes of conduct, 164
Coelho, Paulo, 131
collaboration, 225–27
Comcast, 206
COMDEX, 52–53
commencement speeches, 42–50, 118
communication skills, 63
compensation negotiations, 210–11
competence, 220
competitiveness, 48–49
confidence, 210–11
Connor, Bull, 37
Consumer Electronics Show, 174–75, *175*
contests, 81–82
continuing education, 47
Coon, David, 12
Covewater Paddle Surf, 33–34
credibility, 206
crime, 31–33
critics, 161
crowdsourcing information, 181
cultural diversity, 80
curiosity, 86
customer feedback, 74
customer service, 94–95, 206. *See also*
    product evangelism.

dBASE, 64
decision-making skills, 7–8, 126–29
Delbourg-Delphis, Marylene, 64–65
Dell Computers, 75
democratized design, 72, 96, 124
demoing products, 190–91
Department of Motor Vehicles, 136
desktop publishing, 73
Digital Research, 60, 61–62
diligence, 213. *See also* work ethic.
disagreement, 71–73
disbelief, suspension of, 184
discrimination, 26, 33
dishonor, 108–11

Disney, Roy, 105
diversity, 80
Dixit, Avinash, 48
Doi, Nelson K., 177–78
Donoghue, Emma, 231
drama, 128–29
Drive (Pink), 71, 235
driving tests, 136–37
drug addiction, 47–48
dry ice bombs, 185, 223–24
Duke Kawa's (jazz band), 4
Dweck, Carol, 38, 236
dyslexia, 142–43

eBay, 86–88, 184
editing, 197, 221, 225–27
education
    and author's children, 140
    and author's family background, 3–5
    and career choice, 39–40
    and childhood mistakes, 16–17
    and college choice, 19–21, 21–23
    commencement speech advice, 42–50
    continuing education, 47
    and hiring process, 56–57
    impact of teachers and coaches, 9–15, 150
    MBA programs, 52, 55, 77–78
    and moral ambiguity, 17–18
    and parental guidance, 19–21
    UCLA MBA program, 77–78
Edu-Ware Services, 52–53, 101
eHarmony, 207
Eilers, Dan, 66
elitism, 191
email practices, 120
embarrassment, 17
empathy, 73, 143
employee recruitment, 71, 79, 141–42,
    222, 235
Enchantment (Kawasaki), *81,* 81–82,
    173, 227
engineering, 75
enthusiasm, 189, 222
entrepreneurship, 31, 70, 85, 99
equipment selection, 161
EvangeList, 66–67
excellence as goal, 73, 211
experimentation, 208
experts and expertise, 76, 115, 123,
    186, 208
exploitation, 81–83, 103

externalities, 177–78
extracurricular activities, 118

Facebook
  and branding, 100
  and negativity, 174
  and political campaigns, 115, 117–18, 123
  and professional profiles, 142
  and social influencers, 206
family and friends
  author's commencement speech advice,
    49–50
  author's immigrant heritage, 1–8
  family background of author,
    1–8, 7
  Fitzpatrick essay, 217–18
  Kot essay, 225–27
  Martinuzzi essay, 211–12
  Nate Kawasaki essay, 223–24
  Nic Kawasaki essay, 213–17
  Noah Kawasaki essay, 221–23
  Nohemi Kawasaki essay, 224–25
  ohana meaning, 209
  and parenting, 131–48
  Stein essay, 210–11
  Welch essay, 218–21
Farrington High School, 10, 31–32
fear, 16–17
Feldhaus, Dan, 12, 19
financial success, 30–31, 70–71
First Sino-Japanese War, 2
Fitzpatrick, Peg, 95–98, 217–18
Fog City Software, 102
football, 19–20, 22, 46–47, 149–50
Foresman, Scott, 192–93
formatting, 197–98
4th Dimension, 64–65
freebies, 206
friends. *See* family and friends.

gambling, 20
Garage.com, 102, 109–10
Gassée, Jean-Louis, 64, 65
Gates, Bill, 85–86
GEM (graphical environment manager), 60
General Electric, 30
General Motors, 176
generosity, 113, 224–25
Genovese, Kitty, 145–46
Getty Images, 107
goals, 30–31, 34, 165

Goodall, Jane, 195–96, *196*
Good Writing: An Informal Manual of Style, 13
Google
  and author's writing career, 219
  and political campaigns, 117, 123
  as research tool, 224
  and social influencers, 206–7
  and uncertainty in tech industry, 183
Graham, Martha, 209
Grand Bazaar, *200*
gratitude, 15, 125, 174
grit, 232
growth mind-set, 232
Gruber, Marty, 78, 79
Guy's Golden Touch, 68, 189, 220

Hakalau Plantation Company, 2
Hamada, Edward, 12, 150
Hamilton, Aran, 121
Hannemann, Mufi, 19
happiness, 44–45
Harada, Mildred, *2, 3*
HarperCollins, 226
Haruo, Katherine, *2*
Hawaii, 1, 6–7
Hawaii Commission on Crime, 101, 177
Hedican, Bret, 152–53
Henkens, Jos, 120
Herczeg Institute on Aging, 18
Hindsights (Rice), 36–37
Hirabayashi, Chikao, 5
Hirabayashi, Ellen, 5
Hirabayashi, Elsie, 5
Hirabayashi, Harriet, 5
Hirabayashi, Jean, 5
Hirabayashi, Lucy, 5
Hirabayashi, Marian, 5
Hirabayashi, Richard, 5
The Hired Executive, 210
hiring process, 51–57
Hiroshima, Japan, 1, 8
Hitler, Adolf, 122
hockey, 150–53, *152,* 155, 213–16
Homebrew Computer Club, 86
homelessness, 217–18
Homes, Hicks, 101
honesty, 57–58, 110–11, 136, 191, 233
Honolulu, Hawaii, 2–3
Honolulu Fire Department, 16
Honolulu Kitchen, 85
honor, 105, 108–10

Horn, Mike, 179
humility, 113–15, 180, 221, 227
hunting, 177–78
Huxley, Aldous, xv

IBM, 75, 188
ice harvesters, 45–46
If You Want to Write (Ueland), 28–30, *29,*
    161, 197, 235
iMac, 67
imagination, 1–8
immigrant background of author, 1–8
Inboard, 222
Indo Board, 159
Influence (Cialdini), 236
influencers, 206–7
innovation, 74, 76, 85–86
inspiration
    author's commencement speech advice,
        42–50
    influential authors, 28–30
    and quitting, 39–42
    and racial prejudice, 33–38
    sources of, 25–28
    and success of others, 30–31
    and traumatic events, 31–33
    and unlikely events, 39
    and victimhood mindset, 36–38
Instagram, 86, 117, 206
instant gratification, 95
Institut Teknologi Bandung, 81
intellectual property lawsuits, 60–61
internet, 183. *See also specific internet*
    companies.
internships, 222–23
'Iolani prep school, 10–14, *12, 13,* 16, 19, 40
iPhones, 75, 170, 189
iPods, 67, 192
iStockphoto, 107
IT infrastructure, 191

Japanese culture, 2, 23
jewelry business, 52, 55–56, 77–80
Jike, Tomoyo, 5
job requirements, 56
Jobs, Steve
    and Apple's turnaround, 70
    and author's career at Apple, 11, 51, *54,* 55,
        57–60, 68–71
    on beginner's attitude, 149
    and humility, 114

illness, 125
    and innovation process, 86
    and iPhone developer policy, 170–71
    and lessons from time at Apple, 73–76
    as mentor, 15
    and NeXT, 68
    and presentation tips, 204
    and product evangelism, 189, 190–91
    and public speaking, 199
    and rebound of Apple, 66, 67
job satisfaction, 70–71
Jordan, Michael, 154
joy, 44–45

Kaaihue, Charles, 12, 150
Kaimuki High School, 31, *32*
Kalakaua Middle School, 10
Kalama, Dave, 158
Kalihi Elementary School, 9–10, *10,* 16
Kalihi Valley, 6, *6*
Karlgaard, Rich, 195
karma, 113, 227, 233
Kato, Russell, 40–41, *41*
Kawasaki, Alma, 2, 213–17
Kawasaki, Beth, 66, 131, 150
Kawasaki, Duke, *2, 3, 134*
Kawasaki, Harold, *2,* 3
Kawasaki, Katherine, 3
Kawasaki, Nathan, *229*
    and author's family life, 132, 133, *134,* 142
    personal essay, 223–24
    sports and athletics, 156, 165
Kawasaki, Nicodemus, *228*
    and author's family life, 132, *134,* 140, 141,
        146, 182, 185
    Salesforce job, 112–13
    sports and athletics, 150, 155, 213–17
Kawasaki, Noah, *228*
    and author's family life, 132, *134,* 136, 182
    personal essay, 221–23
    sports and athletics, 150, 155, 216
Kawasaki, Nohemi, *229*
    and author's family life, 132–33, *134,*
        137–39, 143–45, *144*
    personal essay, 224–25
    sports and athletics, 155, 156, *159,* 165
Kawasaki, Richard, *2,* 3
Kawasaki, Yonetaro, *2,* 3
Kawata, Carol, 27
Kawata, Nobuyuki, 27
Kay, John, 12

Keables, Harold, 12–14, *13*, 15
King, Stephen, 187
Kitschke, Zach, 95–97
Kiyosaki, Robert, 194, *194*
Knoware, 57, 58
Kodak, 90
Kona, Hawaii, 2
Kopp-Duller, Astrid, 142
Kot, Rick, 225–27
KPMG, 91
Kurtzig, Sandy, 30–31

The Last Mile program, 172
Lavorato, Pete, 150
law school, 39–41, 45
lawsuits, 110
The Leader as a Mensch (Martinuzzi), 211–12
Lee, Bruce, 77
Lee, William, 12
Letterman, David, 203
Lewis, C. S., 9
Lieberman, Mike, 54
life tests, 126–29
Lindros, Eris, 151–52, *152*
LinkedIn, 73, 100, 123, 141, 202, 206
literary agents, 110
Livingston, Bruce, 107
Lombardo, Carmen, 4, *4*
Lombardo, Guy, 4, *4*, 147
Lomranz, Jacob, 18
Looker, 222
Lor, Patrick, 107
Lotus Development Corporation, 62, 63
luck, 137
Lundrigan, Ed, 121
Lyft, 89–90, 93
lying, 191, 233

Macintosh computers
    and Apple's turnaround, 70
    and author's career trajectory, 54, *54, 55,*
        56, 58–60, 191–92
    and Benioff's career, 111–12
    key evangelists, *52*
    and potential markets, 91
    and product enthusiasts, 66, 83
    and product evangelism, 188, 211–12,
        226–27
    and product value, 75
The Macintosh Way (Kawasaki), 29, 65,
    192–93, 199, 226

MacPaint, 52
Mac Plus, 192
Macworld, 84
MacWrite, 52
Management Science America, 54
manapua, fried, 85, 87
Maple Leaf Foods, 121
marketing, 59–60, 75, 87, 176–77
marriage, 48
Martinuzzi, Bruna, 211–12
Marwick, Peat, 91, 92
materialism, 44
Mavericks, 156
Mayall, Will, 64, 201
MBA programs, 52, 55, 77–78
McCain, Mike, 121
McGee, Kainoa, 155, 157, 162
McGill, Archie, 58
Meiji period (Japan), 1–2
Ménière's disease, 124–25
Mercedes-Benz, 77, 94, 100, 102–3, 122–24,
    178–79
meritocracy, 124
Microsoft, 60, 62–63, 85–86, 117, 158
Microsoft Word, 197–98
Milne, A. A., 167
Mindset (Dweck), 38, 236
minimalist aesthetic, 74
mistakes, 171, 185–86
Moby Dick 1 (surfboard), 160, *160*
Modeste, Mark, 150
morality, 49, 123–24
Moritz, Michael, 181–82
motivation, 33, 71
Motorola, 102
MS-DOS, 188, 190
Murray, Mike, 59–60
musical skill and talent, 3–4, 46
Musk, Elon, 184

Nakamura, Lynn, 78
Nalebuff, Barry, 48
National Grocery Conference, 121
naysayers, 161
neatness, 5
negativity and negative experiences, 32–33,
    174–77, 233
negotiation tactics, 61–62, 210–11
nepotism, 54, 101–2, 113
networking, 103
Nike, 107

Nold, Calder, 156, 158, *160*, 162, 165
"Nova," 176
Nova Stylings, 78–79, 101
NPR, 126–27, 207

Obama, Barack, 1, 10, 19–20, 115
obedience, 16–17
Obrecht, Cliff, 95–97, *96*
Occam's Razor, 169
Occidental College, 19, 20
Office of the Ombudsman, 5
Okimoto, Jean, 5, 6
Omidyar, Pierre, 87
Ondrej Nepela Arena, 151
O'Neill (company), 200, 222
O'Neill, Pat, 200
online marketplaces, 184
opportunity, 8, 81–83
optimism, 111
origami, 7
The Other Guy (Kawasaki), 226
O'Toole, Tom, 89
"outside the box" thinking, 161

paddleboarding, 33–34, 154–62. *See also*
    surfing.
PageMaker, 72
Palo Alto High School, 42, 118
Palo Alto Research Center, 61
The Paper Chase (television series), 40
parenting and parental advice
    and adoption, 133–36
    and author's background, 5–6, 131–33
    and author's commencement speech, 50
    and career advice, 141–42
    and daughters, 143–45
    and discipline, 16–17
    and driving tests, 136–37
    and education of children, 10–11,
        19–21, 23
    and empathy, 142–43, 147–48
    and helping others, 143–45
    illusion of control, 139
    involvement in kids' lives, 213–17
    limits of parental influence, 140–41
    and quitting, 39–41, 42
    and sports, 160
    and teaching positivity, 36
    time and financial challenges,
        137–39
passion, 83–85, 147, 160

passive voice, 14, 198
patience, 15
Peachtree software, 54
Pearl Harbor, 5
Pearson, Bob, 159, *160*
pedigrees, 191
Pemex, 176
Penguin Books, 225–27
penmanship, 14
Pentagon Mac Users Group, 83
perfect information fallacy, 180–81
Perkins, Melanie, 95–97, *96*
perseverance, 15, 232. *See also* work ethic.
personal interests, 85
philanthropy, 112
Pink, Daniel, 71, 235
pitching products and companies, 87, 89, 101,
    103, 125, 188, 190. *See also* product
    evangelism.
Pleasure Point, Santa Cruz, 33, 156–57, 159
Polaroid, 90
positivity, 36, 207, 233
possibilities, 39
PostScript, 72
PowerPoint, 201, 211–12
Pratchett, Terry, xiii
prejudice, 34–36. *See also* racism and racial
    prejudice.
preparation, 137
presentation skills, 200–1, 203–4. *See also*
    public speaking.
pricing practices, 59, 75, 87
priorities, 120
Privy app, 87
Proctor, Charles, 12
product evangelism
    and author's career at Apple, 54, 67–68,
        188–89, 189–92
    and author's writing career, 226–27
    key Macintosh evangelists, *52*
prone surfing, 155–59, 162
public relations, 87
public speaking, 42–50, 199–204
public transit, 93
publishing career of author, 193
Punahou prep school, 10

quality, 189
Quantum Computer Services, 106
quitting, 39–42, 62–63, 65, 68–70
Quora, 137

racism and racial prejudice, 33–37, *37,* 72
reading, 197
reciprocation, 113
"reference-account" concept, 90–91
regression to the mean, 153–54
relationships, cultivating, 128
repetition, 208
reputation, 127–28
re-share test, 127–28
#resist movement, 123
Reynolds, Russell, 102
Ribardière, Laurent, 64–65
Rice, Condoleeza, 36–38
Rich Dad Poor Dad (Kiyosaki),
    194–95
riptides, 146, 164
RISE tech conference, 178
Rogers, Marc, 150
Roizen, Heidi, 168
Rosen, Emmanuel, 236
Rossman, Alain, *52*
rules, 165
Russia, *203*
Russo-Japanese War, 2

safety, 224
salaries, 70–71, 210–11
Salesforce.com, 112
salesmanship, 55, 77–80, *79,* 95. *See also*
    product evangelism.
San Quentin State Prison, 171–74
Santa Cruz, 222–23
scholarships, 19–20
School of Psychological Sciences, 18
Scoble, Robert, *172, 173*
Sculley, John, 64–65
search engines, 183
"second followers," 90–92
Second Peak, 156
segregation, 37
self-doubt, 161
self-esteem, 47
self-improvement, 48–49
Sequoia Capital, 182
serendipity, 87
sharing, 8, 11, 165
shoplifting, 17–18
Shopping Center Test, 128
Silicon Beach Software, 62
Simonson, Itamar, 236
simplicity, 167–69

Sinek, Simon, 90–91
skateboards, 222
skepticism, 186, 233
skills
    and appropriate equipment, 156–61
    cultivating valuable skills, 231–32
    and product evangelism, 188–92
    and public speaking, 199–204
    and regression to the mean,
       153–54
    and social media, 204–7
    See also writing tips and skills.
small changes, 92–93
smiling, 232
Snopes, 176
sociability, 201–2, 224–25
social media
    and ignoring the inconsequential, 100
    and negativity, 174–75
    and political campaigns,
       116–18, 123
    and professional profiles, 141–42
    and re-share test, 127–28
    and social influencers, 204–7
    and writing tips, 198
social networking, 221–23
software development, 59
So-What? Test, 128, 129
speaking agents, 108–11, *110*
speaking engagements, 201–4, 210
"spec" work, 81–82
sports and athletics
    football, 19–20, 22, 46–47,
       149–50
    hockey, 150–53, *152,* 155, 213–16
    involvement in kids' lives, 213–17
    surfing, 147–48, 154–62, *159, 160,* 200,
       216, 222, 224–25
Square, Inc., 218
stand-up paddleboards (SUPs), 155, *158,*
    159, 160
Stanford Medical Center, 27, 40
Stanford Music Library, 101, 103
Stanford University, 10, 19–22, 26–27, 30,
    37, 118, 150
Starboard, 33–34
start-up companies, 33, 92, 98–99,
    132, 227
Start with Why (Sinek), 90–91
Stastny, Peter, 151
Stein, Craig, 210–11

stereotypes, 34–36
stock options, 96–97, 106
stock photography, 107
stories, power of, 87–88, 204
strategic decisions, 92
strength, 169–71
superstition, 154
surfing
    and appropriate equipment,
        156–61, *160*
    and author's daughter, 147–48
    and author's family life, 216, 222,
        224–25
    and involvement in kids' lives, 216
    learning later in life, 154–62,
        158, 159
suspension of disbelief, 184
SXSW, 94, 103, 195

taxi companies, 89–90
teachers, 10–11, 12–14, 15
TED events, 83, 90, 204
Telos, 62
tenacity, 15, 232. *See also* work ethic.
Thaler, Richard, 93
theft, 31–33
thoughtfulness, 217–18
Tinder, 207
tinnitus, 124–25
titles, 191
Tivol of Kansas City, 79
T/Maker, 62
Tomita, Harry, *2, 3*
Tomson, Shaun, 162, *163,* 164
tourism, 119
transparency, 207
travel, 119, 200–1, *203*
Trump, Donald, 115, 122
trust, 60, 79
truthfulness, 57–58, 110–11, 136, 191, 233.
    See also honesty.
Turkcell, 19
Twitter
    and author's writing career, 217
    and Canva, 97
    and political campaigns, 117, 123
    and social influencers, 204–5,
        206–7

Ueland, Brenda, 28, 161, 197, 235
unique skills, 231–32

United Airlines, 89, 114
University of California, Berkeley, 140
University of California, Los Angeles
    (UCLA), 27, 30, 77–78, 140
University of Hawaii (UH), 10, 19, 20
University of Southern California
    (USC), 111
US Air Force, 84

validation, 92
values
    accepting help, 115–18
    avoiding drama, 128–29
    and Canadians, 121–22
    generosity, 111–13
    honor, 105–8, 108–11
    humility, 113–15
    and political beliefs, 122–26
    priorities, 120
    and providing value to others,
        126–28, 207
    and travel, 118–19
VanMoof, 93
Vargas, Sandi, 131
venture capital, 109–10, 181–82, 184
verification, 110
Viagra, 86
victimhood, 36–38
Virgin America, 114–15
Vrooman, Alan, 13
vulnerability, 169–71

Ward, William Arthur, xvii
Warnock, John, 72
Waze, 181
weakness, 169–71
Web 2.0, 170
Welch, Shawn, 218–21
What the Plus! (Kawasaki), 219
Wikimedia Foundation, 167–69, 205
Wikipedia, 126, 127, 226
Wilde, Oscar, 25
Windows, 204
Winer, Dave, *172,* 173
winning as a means, 48–49
Wise Guy (Kawasaki), 226
Wolfe, Tom, 195
Woodside Priory, 140
word processing, 14, 52–53, 71–73
work ethic, 13, 56, 118, 176,
    213, 232

work experience, 56–57
World War II, 8, 23
Wozniak, Steve, 86
writing tips and skills
  adjectives vs. stories, 87–88, 204
  author's first book, 65
  author's writing career, 192–96
  avoiding adverbs, 14, 198
  avoiding passive voice, 14, 198
  and collaboration, 219, 226–27
  influential authors, 28–30, 161,
    197, 235
  influential teachers, 13–14

  key tips, 197–98
  and word processing, 14, 52–53, 71–73

Xerox, 61

Yahoo!, 181–84
Yamaguchi, Kristi, 152–53
Yelas, Joseph, 12, 150
Yocam, Del, 62, 63, 64–65
YouTube, 183

Zatoichi, 169–70
Zetsche, Dieter, 94, 178–79